THE GOSPEL THAT
JESUS PREACHED

THE GOSPEL
THAT JESUS PREACHED

AND THE GOSPEL FOR TO-DAY

BY

A. T. CADOUX
B.A. (Good Hope), D.D. (London)

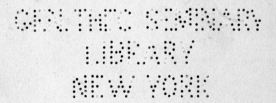

LONDON: GEORGE ALLEN & UNWIN LTD.
RUSKIN HOUSE, 40 MUSEUM STREET, W.C.1

First published in 1925

ALFRED A. KNOPF
LIBRARY
NEW YORK

Printed in Great Britain

THIS BOOK

IS

DEDICATED

TO

C. JOHN CADOUX,

MY BROTHER AND FRIEND,

AND TO

W. DAVID FFRENCH,

MY FRIEND AND COUNSELLOR HEREIN

CONTENTS

CHAPTER I

CHAPTER II

CHAPTER III

CHAPTER IV

CHAPTER V

CONTENTS

9

PAGEPAGE

CHAPTER VI

The Gospel that Jesus Preached

and

The Gospel for To-day

CHAPTER I

INTRODUCTORY

THE Christian Church claims, and has always claimed, to have a gospel. She asserts, as her right to exist, that she has a truth to proclaim, a truth which, if men accept it, gives them a lasting, great, energizing, transforming joy. She offers the world what she avers to be life's greatest gift.

But what is this life-transforming truth? Traditional Christianity defines the gospel as the forgiveness of sins through faith in the death of Jesus. A strictly worded definition might use other terms, but we find the stricter definitions varying from age to age, and it is doubtful whether the traditional gospel of the Christian Church for the last eighteen centuries could be put more fairly in words other than these. At least they represent tolerably what most Christian people to-day mean by " the gospel."

And yet it cannot be denied that the gospel, understood in this way, is losing its power to make a transforming difference to the man who accepts it. Most Christian people to-day would confess with sincerity that they believed their sins to be forgiven through faith in the death of Jesus, but comparatively few would experience any exuberance of joy in the confession. It was not always so, and even to-day there are exceptions; for if a man finds in the traditional gospel the only escape from endless and measureless torment, it may well· be to him a perpetual joy. And we remember that throughout the whole of its long course the traditional gospel has had, as its presupposition and ground of appeal, the firm conviction that it provided the only escape from eternal anguish. Nor can this conviction be removed without revolutionary reaction upon the gospel which rested on it.

And no fact of modern religious life is plainer than that fewer and fewer Christians believe in a hereafter of endless torment. They find such a doom incompatible with the goodness of God. It pushes the penalty of wrong-doing to the point at which the judge himself becomes unjust. An adequate imagination of such a future produces an overwhelming fear and paralyses moral choice. But it is needless to multiply these considerations : the fact is with us, that hell in the sense that gave force to the traditional gospel has ceased to be a factor in the religion of a very large number of people. And with the loss of this factor the traditional gospel inevitably loses much of its power.

The fear of endless and unspeakable misery as the result of dying unforgiven has for so long almost monopolized the interest in forgiveness that when this fear ceases to operate, forgiveness becomes a pale and minor boon. Though there still remains belief in a just punishment for sin, there is growing repugnance to the idea that forgiveness means release from merited penalty. On the one hand, the wish to escape just punishment seems mean and cowardly, while, on the other, we are sure that God in His goodness will do only what is best for us.

Forgiveness, of course, is something more than remission of penalty : we are often constrained to ask pardon where we do not fear punishment. But although we are sharply aware that we have harmed our fellows and therefore need forgiveness from them, we find it very difficult to feel that our wrong-doing has done real hurt to God and therefore needs His forgiveness.

And then, too, Christendom's growing interest in the teaching of Jesus suggests that forgiveness,— when we do feel our need of it,—is to be obtained in ways that are not obviously connected with the traditional gospel. For the reiterated and unmistakably clear teaching of Jesus on the matter is that God forgives when men ask forgiveness, provided they are willing to forgive their fellows.

The change of Christian thought about future punishment is sufficient to account for the growing inefficiency of the traditional gospel. And an inefficiency in the Church's gospel is more than enough to explain the slackening of her hold on the life of the people. Nor has a remedy been found in the many recent attempts to restate the gospel in terms that are free from objectionable presuppositions. None of them has recaptured the effectiveness of the traditional gospel. The reason seems to be that their authors have not fully recognized all that is involved in the abandonment of the idea of eternal torment. For when escape from punishment ceases to be the dominant interest in religion, then forgiveness can no longer be the central element of the gospel, and therefore no modification of the terms and pre-suppositions of forgiveness can meet the need of the changed conditions. An instance will make this clear.

When we say that, the fear of hell having gone, forgiveness loses its urgency because it is not easy to feel that our sin has done hurt to God, we shall be told that our difficulty is due to an insufficient notion of God's love, for, if we understood its greatness, we should know that our sin was a pain and a loss to Him. And when we say that it is precisely our difficulty that we find it hard to believe feelingly that God loves us to that extent, then we are told that in the cross of Christ we shall find what our sin means to the love of God. This we believe, but just so far as it is true, it presupposes the gospel to be something other than forgiveness through the death of Jesus. For unless we can think of God as loving unrepentant sinners, we cannot think of our sin as hurting Him and therefore as needing His forgiveness; but we know of such love in God only when we believe we see His love in the cross of Christ, and it is precisely this belief that reconciles us to God. That is, we are without such knowledge of God as makes us know that we have sinned against Him and need His forgiveness until we have the very knowledge that reconciles us to Him. It thus becomes evident that something other than, and prior to, forgiveness is the true centre of the gospel.

In any presentation of the gospel the possibility and value of forgiveness must depend ultimately upon what is believed about God. This grows very obvious when the fear of punishment is no longer dominant. For unless we believe that God loves us we cannot feel that our sin has wronged Him; in which case our desire for forgiveness would disappear when we no longer feared punishment. But when we have found God's goodness to be of the sort that makes sin against Him a biting reality, we have already solved the problem of forgiveness, for the love that suffers knows how to pardon.

We are therefore driven to the conclusion that the only form of gospel that can be effective to-day must be somewhat as follows : that, because of all that Jesus was, His thought of God may be ours. And we at once see that this replaces the traditional gospel with one that is very much nearer the gospel which Jesus Himself preached.

Such a gospel demands no presuppositions. It is simply and directly communicable. But its vindication demands a certain line of treatment. We must first make good the assertion that it represents the gospel that Jesus preached (Chapter II). Then we must examine the objection that such a gospel is not the gospel of Paul and of other writers of the New Testament (Chapter III). The fourth chapter recounts the experience which compelled the author of this book so to understand the gospel of Jesus ; and some readers may be satisfied with having pursued the subject so far. But, since an essential part of this gospel is that it creates rather than presupposes a belief in God, two more points are involved : it will be necessary to examine the validity of the faith thus created (Chapter V) and its reflection upon certain elements in theology (Chapter VI).

It will be observed that the greater part of the book is a vindication of this gospel against various tenets which are incompatible with it, and the reader must not allow the exigencies of defence to obscure the simplicity and directness of the gospel itself.

CHAPTER II

THE GOSPEL THAT JESUS PREACHED

(1)

To say that the Christian Gospel is that Jesus' thought of God may be ours, rather than that we may have forgiveness through His death, is bound to rouse objection. Such an interpretation will be charged with slighting the long-cherished tradition of the Church, and will be said to assume that the earliest followers of Jesus misunderstood Him.

With regard to the second point we shall see in the next chapter that while the traditional gospel has the appearance of maintaining continuity with certain elements in Pauline epistles and other books of the New Testament, it ignores their more fundamental and vital elements, which are one with the gospel that Jesus preached.

But the charge that in proposing such a rewording of the gospel we are breaking recklessly with traditional Christianity can come with consistency only from those who still hold to the doctrine of endless torment. For that tenet has been one of the few elements of the traditional gospel about which the thought of the Church has been stable. On the question as to how the death of Jesus saves men, the thought of the Church has differed from age to age, but it has been comparatively constant as to what it saved them from. So that when once we abandon faith in the finality of hell we have already broken with the most consistent element in the traditional gospel.

And it is beyond the possibility of question that Jesus had a gospel which He preached and that His gospel was not the traditional gospel and was very different from it. Much of the evidence of this will be reserved for the next chapter (see especially pp. 87–95), and it will be enough in the meantime to recall certain outstanding facts, confining ourselves to the material of the first three gospels, since in the present state of criticism the Fourth Gospel cannot be claimed to rank with them as direct evidence for the sayings and deeds of Jesus. The names Matthew, Mark, Luke and John will for convenience' sake be used to designate the gospels, but this should not be taken as involving the acceptance of any particular theory of authorship.

On reading the first three Gospels we at once see that the traditional gospel must have broken very completely with the gospel of Jesus. The traditional gospel is that we may have forgiveness of sins through the death of Jesus : Jesus preached His gospel (Mark i. 14, 15) before the time when He began to speak of His death to His followers (Mark viii. 31) : He pronounced forgiveness of sins without any condition of faith in His death and before He had made any mention of it (Mark ii. 5, Luke vii. 47) : He spoke much of forgiveness and of conditions of forgiveness without any reference to His death, the only condition on which He insisted being that we should forgive our fellows (Matt. vi. 14, 15 ; Mark xi. 25, etc.).

Another obvious and significant difference is that the gospel of Jesus is essentially the gospel of the kingdom of God (Matt. iv. 23, Mark i. 14, 15, etc.), a term easily and often omitted from the proclamation and exposition of the traditional gospel. And among the many things that Jesus said about fitness for the kingdom of God there is nothing like the demand for faith in His death which the traditional gospel makes the one essential condition of salvation (cf. Matt. v. 3, 10 ; Mark x. 15, Luke ix. 62). In the parable of the two debtors (Matt. xviii. 23 ff.), where He deals expressly with the kingdom of heaven as it touches God's forgiveness of sins, He repeats His central teaching on this matter, that the one necessary condition is that we forgive others.

The second dominant theme of Jesus' teaching, the fatherhood of God, fares little better in the traditional gospel. It is true that most theories of atonement claim to illustrate the love of God, but the necessity for atonement is generally based on some other attribute of God than His love. There is no doubt that the common effect of the traditional gospel is to make the love of Jesus Christ appear purer, more intense and unselfish than the love of God. And when we add to this the essential part that the doctrine of endless torment played in the traditional gospel, we cannot be surprised that the fatherhood of God became a much modified and attenuated thought. It is noticeable that this doctrine produces a tendency to worship the divinity of love rather in the Virgin Mary or in Jesus than in God.

If, therefore, it is said that our interpretation of the gospel breaks away from the long-cherished tradition of the Church, we are justified in replying that the traditional gospel broke away from the gospel of Jesus. Nor would it be difficult to find those who acknowledge this and maintain quite frankly that the traditional gospel is not only different from the gospel that Jesus preached but superior to it. They argue that, since remission of sin through the death of

Jesus is the true gospel, it was clearly impossible that it should be preached before Jesus died and that the gospel He preached could not have been the gospel in the true and specially Christian sense, but must have been something of a partial, preliminary nature. Nor do they regard this as a slur upon His work, for they hold that He came rather to die than to teach or preach. But if we accept both their appraisal of the traditional gospel as the only way of salvation and their assertion that it did not exist until Jesus died, we are left unable to attribute to Jesus anything that could be called a gospel at all, since according to their thought a man might accept the gospel of Jesus and be still unsaved. If they are right, then Jesus not only preached a gospel that was not worth the name, but His teaching with regard to forgiveness was very misleading on a point vital to man's salvation.

It may perhaps be suspected that the Church's later activities in preaching the gospel caused a similar activity to be attributed to Jesus, and the emphasis of Mark on the gospel has been debited to Pauline influence. But if the Church had a gospel while Jesus had none, it must have been because without His death there could be no gospel. Hence if the early Church attributed a fictitious gospel to Jesus we should expect to find it closely connected with His predictions of His death, whereas the evangelists tell us that Jesus preached His gospel long before He began to speak of His death (Mark i. 14, 15 ; viii. 31). Subsequent developments may have had some influence on the record in its account of the nature of Jesus' gospel (as, e.g., in Mark i. 15, where " the time is fulfilled " may possibly, though by no means necessarily, be due to Pauline influence), but there is no good reason for doubting the substantial truth of the evangelists' picture of Jesus as the preacher of a gospel.

Of course, the words " preach " and " gospel," so common in the first three gospels, must not in this connection be unduly strained. But they are important because they connote something more than teaching. Teaching may concern the relatively unimportant or that on which the teacher's mind is in abeyance. Preaching is always the preacher's conviction upon the most important issue of the moment. A gospel is more than instruction : it is the announcement of a blessedly revolutionary truth. Confucius was a great teacher, but it would be incongruous to speak of him as the preacher of a gospel in the sense in which we use the term of Jesus or of Paul.

And the record of Jesus' words evinces this gospel quality. He offered to men an incomparable and transforming boon. We have this in the parable of the hidden treasure (Matt. xiii. 44), in the invitation ' Come unto Me . . . and I will give you rest " (Matt. xi. 28), and more clearly still in His declaration that though John was the greatest of woman born he was less than the least in the kingdom of God (Matt. xi. 11, Luke vii. 28).

The supreme importance of His message is expressed in such sayings as, " Whosoever he be of you that renounceth not all that he hath, he cannot be My disciple " (Luke xiv. 33) ; " He that doth not take his cross and follow after Me, is not worthy of Me " (Matt. x. 38) ; " If any man would come after Me, let him deny himself and take up his cross, and follow Me " (Mark viii. 34, Matt. xvi. 24, Luke ix. 23). Jesus could not have spoken so, had He regarded the gospel He preached as incomplete and preliminary to the real gospel which could not be preached till after His death. It is abundantly clear that He had no doubt as to the finality of His own message. In the parable of the Sower there is no hint that the seed is a temporary substitute soon to be superseded by the really effective truth. In reply to the ruler's question, " What shall I do that I may inherit eternal life ? " Jesus does not refer him to some gospel to be preached in the future,—the one thing lacking could be had then and there (Mark x. 17–21). In the parable of the Two Builders we have Jesus' estimate of the finality of His own words in the salvation of men,—the final criterion of sound and unsound life is to be found in relationship, not to a gospel that could not be preached until after His death, but to " these words of Mine " (Matt. vii. 24–27, Luke vi. 46–49). So too in Mark viii. 35 we have His gospel again as the final criterion of salvation : " Whosoever shall lose his life for My sake and the gospel's shall save it."

The gospel that Jesus preached is generally described in the New Testament as " the gospel of the kingdom of God " (or " of heaven "), and the accuracy of the phrase is confirmed by the central place which the kingdom of God occupies in His teaching. There can be little doubt that, despite its possibly Pauline form, Mark's account is substantially correct, " Jesus came . . . preaching the gospel of God, and saying, The time is fulfilled, and the kingdom of God is at hand : repent ye, and believe in the gospel " (Mark i. 14, 15).

But what did Jesus mean by " the kingdom of God " ? It is unnecessary to enter here into the now obsolescent controversy raised by the " eschatological school " of New Testament scholars. Jesus undoubtedly looked for future history to vindicate His truth, and it is probable that, latterly at least, He expected a speedy and catastrophic end to the age in which He lived ; but that He understood by this what we understand by " the end of the world " is more than doubtful, while the catastrophe that within forty years of His death befell Israel at the hand of Rome may well have been an important element in that which He foresaw and foretold. In any case many of His best attested sayings show that in His thought of " the kingdom of God," a world-ending catastrophe was not the dominant element.

It is to be noted that in Jesus' teaching the term " kingdom of God " does not occur in connection with catastrophic eschatology. There are only two apparent exceptions. In one we have Luke's modification (Luke xxi. 31) of Mark (xiii. 29), so that it belongs rather to the evangelist than to his Master, while in the other case (Mark ix. 1) the term is itself specially modified and the context does not at all necessarily bear a catastrophic sense : " Verily I say unto you, There be some here of them that stand by, which shall in no wise taste of death, till they see the kingdom of God come *with power*."

Jesus undoubtedly looked for a future consummation of the kingdom of God, but it is quite as certain that He thought of it as a present factor in the world. The saying that since the days of John the kingdom of God had " suffered violence " (Matt. xi. 12, Luke xvi. 16), whatever it may mean, has otherwise no meaning at all.

The parables of the leaven (Matt. xiii. 33, Luke xiii. 20) and of the mustard-seed (Matt. xiii. 31 f., Mark iv. 30 ff., Luke xiii. 18 f.) show the kingdom of God as a gradual development, while that of the growing corn (Mark iv. 26–29) unites both the gradual and the sudden. In this connection the picture of the future in Matt. viii. 11 (Luke xiii. 28), which shows us Abraham and Isaac and Jacob in the kingdom of God, may be compared with the saying that he that

is but little in the kingdom of God is greater than
John (Matt. xi. 11, Luke vii. 28). For where there
was room for Jacob, Jesus would certainly not have
excluded the prophet whom He called the greatest
born of woman ; so that in these two sayings we have
two distinct and contrasted aspects of the kingdom,
one present and the other future.

Whatever Jesus may have thought of the future,
the important thing to Him was undoubtedly the
relationship of men to God in the present. Whatever
visible, historic vindication the future might hold for
the kingship of God, the characteristic of His message
was the present possibility of entering the kingdom
and possessing its blessedness,—" The kingdom of
God cometh not with observation : neither shall
they say, Lo, here ! or, There ! for lo, the kingdom
of God is within (or amongst) you " (Luke xvii. 20 f.).
In some of the beatitudes the kingdom of heaven is
spoken of as a present possession (Matt. v. 3, 10 ;
Luke vi. 20) in contrast to others in which it is a
future blessing (Matt. v. 4, 5, 6), and it is to be noted
that only the former has the attestation of both
gospels. Jesus' charge against Israel's teachers was
that they hindered those who were entering in
(Matt. xxiii. 13). The kingdom of God was to Jesus
the goal of human effort, not its supersession by
divine intervention : " Seek ye first the kingdom of
God " (Matt. vi. 33, Luke xii. 31), and Jesus stresses
the need for human endeavour here : " Strive ye to
enter in " (Luke xiii. 24 ; cf. Matt. vii. 13 and Mark ix.
47 with its parallels). All this tends to show that
when Jesus declared that the kingdom of God was
" at hand " He meant rather possibility in the present
than actuality in the near future. Only in the sense
of a present possibility could He have said to the
Jews, " The kingdom of God shall be taken away

from you, and shall be given to a nation bringing
forth the fruits thereof " (Matt. xxi. 43).

These considerations compel us to recognize that
our word " kingdom " does not do full justice to the
Jewish idea which it represents, an important element
of which was the more ethical and spiritual notion of
" kingship." The inadequacy of the word " kingdom " is seen in a passage of the most Jewish book
of the New Testament : " I John, your brother and
partaker with you in the tribulation and kingdom
and patience which are in Jesus " (Rev. i. 9). And
such a parable as that of the two debtors (Matt. xviii.
23 ff.) is a figure of God's kingship rather than His
kingdom. Though the kingdom of God is specifically
a community, that which constitutes this community
and distinguishes it from others is the kingship of
God in the hearts of its members.

And we see clearly that if the nearness of God's
kingdom is to be a gospel, then " kingdom " must be
understood mainly as moral and spiritual kingship.
For the vindication of God's kingship by the destruction of the wicked might have been a gospel to others
but not to Jesus, and the only alternative to such a
vindication lies in the acceptance of the spiritual
kingship of God. All that we know of Jesus makes it
sure that He could not have preached the nearness of
the kingdom of God as glad tidings unless it meant
the present possibility of God's kingship in human
hearts. And all that He said with regard to entrance
into the kingdom of God confirms this assumption.
Those who enter must be as little children (Matt. xviii. 3,
Mark x. 15, Luke xviii. 17) : must have a righteousness beyond that of the Pharisees (Matt. v. 20) :
must be doers of God's will (Matt. vii. 21) : must be
wholehearted in their service (Luke ix. 62).

And this carries us to the recognition of another

feature. The kingship of God that Jesus sought was the voluntary, glad, trustful obedience of man. "The sons of the kingdom" "are free" (Matt. xvii. 26). Jesus' idea of kingship involves this; for if kingship lies in the king's service of the subject (Mark ix. 35, x. 42–44, with the Matthæan and Lucan parallels), then the true response of the subject must lie in his willing concurrence with the king. Other sorts of obedience are condemned by Jesus in the figures of the man who hid his lord's talent and the labourers who bargained with their employer. The labourer who "for joy" sells all and buys the treasure-trove is Jesus' picture of man's right enthronement of God (Matt. xiii. 44). In contrasting the enforced kingship of Gentile rulers with the kingdom of God, Jesus spoke of His death as a ransom which would enfranchise His followers (Mark x. 45), implying that at all costs the obedience of the kingdom of God must be free.

From all these considerations it follows that if God is to have that kingship in the human heart which He desires, man must know the truth about God. Man will not serve God freely unless he knows God truly. This appears in the two parables already cited, those of the talents and vineyard-labourers (Matt. xxv. 14 ff., Luke xix. 11 ff., Matt. xx. 1 ff.), in both of which the service that God wants from man is shown to depend upon a right understanding of the character of God. The relationship of truth to the kingdom of God is seen, but less clearly, in the saying, "Every scribe who hath been made a disciple of the kingdom of heaven is like unto a man that is a householder, which bringeth out of his treasure things new and old" (Matt. xiii. 52). It is clearer in "Woe unto you, scribes and Pharisees, hypocrites! because ye shut the kingdom of heaven against men: for ye

enter not in yourselves, neither suffer ye them that
are entering in to enter " (Matt. xxiii. 13), especially
as compared with the Lucan version : " Woe unto you,
lawyers ! for ye took away the key of knowledge : ye
entered not in yourselves, and them that were entering
in ye hindered " (Luke xi. 52). And in John xviii. 37
Jesus tells Pilate that it was the purpose of His life to
" bear witness to the truth."

We here see the vital connection between the two
great terms of Jesus' teaching, " the kingdom of
God " and " your heavenly Father." The inward
side of His proclamation of the nearness of the
kingdom of heaven is that He could give man such a
thought of God as would enthrone God in the hearts
of all who accepted His truth.

The dependence of the kingdom of God upon our
thought of God finds chief expression in two very
significant places. When the lawyer agreed that what
God wants most from men is love for Himself and for
their fellows, Jesus pronounced him to be " not far
from the kingdom of God " (Mark xii. 34). More
significant still is the prayer, " Father, hallowed be
Thy name, Thy kingdom come " (Luke xi. 2,
Matt. vi. 9, 10),—the understanding of God's character,
i.e. the giving of a right meaning to His name, must
be the prelude to the coming of His kingdom.

But there is evidence that He found this enthroning
truth of God bound up with His own consciousness
and life : He Himself was in word and act its instance
and evidence. The classical expression of this is in
the saying, " All things have been delivered unto Me
of My Father, and no one knoweth the Son save the
Father ; neither doth any know the Father save the
Son, and he to whomsoever the Son willeth to reveal
Him " (Matt. xi. 27, Luke x. 22). In these words
Jesus speaks of Himself as Son of God in the sense of

having a unique knowledge of God together with the power of imparting that knowledge to others. Their authenticity has been challenged largely because their style is that of the Fourth Gospel rather than that of the first three. But they do no more than make explicit what is involved in other expressions and experiences of His life. They give the inwardness of the experience at baptism when He heard the voice, " Thou art My beloved Son, in Thee I am well pleased " (Mark i. 11), for these words, too, express Jesus' consciousness of unique knowledge of God, a consciousness that may well have had its occasion in the comparison of His own thought of God with that of the Baptist, the greatest of those outside the kingdom. The baptism is followed immediately by the temptations, which turn on the validity of this consciousness, " If Thou art the Son of God," and on the nature of the acts that should express it. And the act in which it does finally express itself is that Jesus became the preacher of the gospel of the kingdom of God. At the crisis of His work we have again, in the story of the transfiguration, the record of the vocally externalized conviction of a sonship uniquely capable of making God known : " This is My beloved Son, hear ye Him " (Mark ix. 7).

And when we turn from these biographical passages and consider Jesus' teaching, we find the same consciousness of being the unique bearer of a unique truth of God of which He Himself was the evidence.

When Galilee rejected His message and He saw Jerusalem and death before Him, when His followers must therefore hold His truth in face of a hostile people, He turns their thoughts to Himself : " Who say ye that I am ? " (Mark viii. 29). And in such sayings as, " Blessed are your eyes . . ." (Matt. xiii.16, 17 ; Luke x. 23, 24), " Unto you is given to know the mystery of the kingdom of God" (Mark iv. 11, Matt. xiii. 11, Luke viii. 10), "A greater (thing) than Jonah is here. . . . A greater (thing) than Solomon is here" (Matt. xii. 41, 42; Luke xi. 31, 32), "A greater (thing) than the temple is here" (Matt. xii. 6), "If I by the finger of God cast out demons, then is the kingdom of God come nigh unto you" (Matt. xii. 28, Luke xi. 20), we have the announcement of something infinitely important to humanity, something not merely Himself but present in His presence. He stands for what ought to take precedence of all other claims,— "He that loveth father or mother more than Me is not worthy of Me; he that loveth son or daughter more than Me is not worthy of Me" (Matt. x. 37, Luke xiv. 26). In the parable of the wicked husbandmen He is Himself the last and dearest messenger of God (Mark xii. 6): He is the rejected stone that will become "the head of the corner" (Mark xii. 10).

We may say, then, that the gospel that Jesus preached was the gospel of a truth of God of such sort that they who accept it gladly enthrone God in their hearts and so enter the kingdom of God; that He was conscious of being unique in possession of this thought and therefore bound to impart it; that He knew Himself to be that which made this conception of God credible to men, and which thus brought God's kingdom near to them. And this tallies tolerably with the description of the gospel to which we were driven in our first chapter.

When we ask what it was that made Jesus' thought of God a gospel, we turn, of course, to His teaching of the fatherhood of God. It may be said that Jesus was not the first to speak of God as Father; but newness, even revolutionary newness, of thought may lie in new meaning and emphasis as well as in new words. When Greek or Roman spoke of the supreme deity as father, it seems to have been little more than an honorific title implying originative and controlling power. And the Gentile world lacked much of the Jewish ideal of fatherhood which gave its peculiar meaning to Jesus' use of the word. The earlier teachers of Israel spoke of God as father of the nation. Jesus spoke of Him as father of the individual, and more significantly made this conception of God central and regulative. To the test of this thought He brought the practical problems of religion and life (Matt. vii. 11, Luke xi. 13). But the inadequacy of even this figure without further determination appears in the words already cited : " No man knoweth the Father save the Son, and he to whom the Son willeth to reveal Him," implying that it was not enough to take the common notion of human fatherliness and apply it to God, but that only in what Jesus Himself would be to His fellows did He find that which satisfied Him as a portrayal of God. So that we are driven back to Jesus Himself for His truth of God in its fulness. Probably, however, we shall not be wrong in finding the characteristics of His thought of God in three passages :—

(1) Mark xii. 28–34 (Matt. xxii. 34–40, Luke x. 25–28), where Jesus says that the greatest command is God's demand for human love.

(2) Luke xv. (Matt. xviii. 12–14), where, in the parable of the lost sheep and lost coin and of the prodigal, God seeks or watches for the wanderer and where God's joy depends upon the finding of the lost.

(3) Matt. v. 43–48 (Luke vi. 27, 28, 32–36), where, in the command to love those who do not love us, we are told to imitate God's love.[1]

[1] We should perhaps note here a not uncommon but quite unnecessary difficulty connected with some of Jesus' parables, in which the figure representing God has traits of character that are unfatherly, as in the treatment of the man without the wedding

(2)

What the death of Jesus has to do with His gospel cannot be fully discussed in this chapter. The effort of His life centred in the attempt to bring Israel to repentance and acceptance of His gospel. The crucifixion was Israel's complete and final rejection of His appeal; and the deepest significance of His suffering lies in His experience of this defeat. Naturally, therefore, this aspect of His death can find little place in His teaching or in any acts except the last. On the other hand, it is clear that the significance of failure depends upon the nature of the attempt. So that, though the death of Jesus takes us to heights and depths greater than His life, its whole significance turns upon the direction of His life's work.

It is in any case clearly wrong to divorce the purpose and meaning of Jesus' death from the historic steps that led to it, as we see them in His own acts and those of others. His death was incurred in pursuit of His life's task, which was to preach the gospel. And so far as Jesus was conscious of a meaning and purpose in His death, it is clear that it must be one with the meaning and purpose of His life. His death is therefore to be understood in the light of His own gospel and not of any other.

These considerations must be borne in mind as we examine the sayings, recorded in the first three Gospels, which seem to throw light upon Jesus' thought of His death.

(*a*)

" Can the sons of the bride-chamber fast, while the bridegroom is with them ? as long as they have the

garment. We have to remember that the parables give analogies of action rather than likeness of character, and may sometimes even give point to the former by contrast in the latter, as where the unjust judge stands for God or where the unjust steward stands for the disciple (Luke xviii. 1–7 and xvi. 1–9).

bridegroom with them, they cannot fast. But the days will come, when the bridegroom shall be taken away from them, and then will they fast in that day" (Mark ii. 19, 20 ; Matt. ix. 15 ; Luke v. 34, 35).

We probably have here Jesus' earliest recorded reference to His death. The word "taken away" does not necessarily imply violence : it would seem applicable to any acutely felt distance, literal or figurative, between Master and disciple, such as occurred towards the end (Mark x. 32, xiv. 19). But the nature and occasion of such instances confirm the natural suggestion that Jesus here refers specially to His death. So understood, the words certainly do not suggest that His disciples must await His death for any real gospel. "Then will they fast in that day," and fasting is not appropriate to the reception of "glad tidings." Nor is it a bridegroom's intention and vocation to be "taken away." The whole figure implies that Jesus regarded His death, not as the fulfilment of some divinely preordained plan, but as the result of an unnecessary and unnatural opposition not less intrusive upon His purpose than a brigand raid upon a bridal feast.

(b)

In Mark viii. 31, ix. 31, x. 33, 34 (with their parallels in Matt. and Luke) we have three accounts of Jesus' teaching as to the death and resurrection of the Son of man, obviously understood as referring to Himself. This repetition and the wording and setting of the three accounts suggest that they are variant traditions of the same event, which was probably a more or less prolonged period of teaching and included the prediction of Mark ix. 12. This last passage is very significant of Jesus' thought with regard to His death, for here, as in Mark xiv. 21, He refers to a scriptural prophecy of the sufferings of the Son of man,—" How is it written of the Son of man, that He should suffer many things ? " " The Son of man goeth, even as it is written of Him." Now the only scripture that can be called a prophecy of the sufferings of the Son of man is Daniel vii., which does claim to be a prediction and where the " Son of man " who receives the kingdom is said to symbolize " the saints of the Most High " and where it is said that their way into the kingdom must be through suffering (Dan. vii. 13, 14, 16, 18, 21–27). It is perverse to insist that when Jesus said, " It is written of the Son of man that He should suffer," He was referring to a scripture like Isa. liii. which does not speak of the " Son of man " and is a record of suffering past, not a prediction of suffering to come. We have surely no warrant for thinking that Jesus was here referring to any other passage than the only one in which it is written of the Son of man that He should suffer. Nor does it mend matters to say that He used the term " Son of man " as simply equivalent to " I," for His use of it is characteristically connected with the prediction of suffering, and where He does refer to Isa. liii. (Luke xxii. 37) He does not use the term " Son of man." We have also to note that the simplest form in which we have Jesus' prediction of His suffering, " The Son of man is delivered up into the hands of men, and they shall kill Him ; and when He is killed, after three days He shall rise again " (Mark ix. 31), is strongly reminiscent of " they shall be given into His hand until a time and times and half a time " (Dan. vii. 25). We note too that the outstanding features of Dan. vii. are outstanding features of Jesus' teaching,—the Son of man and the kingdom of God. Nor is it possible to deny the influence of Dan. vii. 13 in such sayings as

Mark viii. 38, xiii. 26, and especially in Jesus' reply to the high priest, " Ye shall see the Son of man sitting at the right hand of power, and coming with the clouds of heaven " (Mark xiv. 62). We cannot, therefore, refuse to regard Dan. vii. as the most important of all Old Testament documents for understanding Jesus' use of the title " Son of man " and especially for His teaching concerning the sufferings of the " Son of man," in which connection, as we have seen, He twice makes specific reference to this scripture.

And the general meaning of Dan. vii., as far as it touches the question in hand, is made clear enough in its visions and interpretations. We have first the vision of the four beasts (vs. 1–12), which passes into the vision of the Son of man, and Daniel is told that the former are four kings (v. 17), while the interpretation of the vision of the Son of man is that " the saints of the Most High shall receive the kingdom, and possess the kingdom for ever." A further vision (vs. 21–22) and interpretation (vs. 23–27) tell him that the reception of the kingdom by the saints of the Most High will be preceded by a time of suffering when they shall be " given into the hand " of a violent and evil power who shall " make war " upon them and " prevail against " them and " wear them out " for " a time and times and half a time," and then " the time came that the saints possessed the kingdom." The " Son of man " who " came with the clouds of heaven " (v. 13) and to whom was given " dominion and glory and a kingdom " (v. 14) thus represents " the saints of the Most High " receiving the eternal kingdom, but before this triumph there is to be a time of oppression and suffering.

Jesus, therefore, by the use He made of the term " Son of man " and by His frequent and obvious references to the visions and interpretations of Dan. vii., especially in connection with His sufferings and death, gives us ground for two conclusions :—

(1) That He regarded His death as a means to the kingdom of God, i.e. as furthering and realizing the kingdom whose nearness was His gospel.

(2) That He thought of Himself in His sufferings as one with " the saints of the Most High," which is the Danielic interpretation of the " Son of man."

(c)

Considering the obviously great importance of the prophecy of Dan. vii. in the thought of Jesus and the number of His sayings that refer to it, and especially considering its unique place in His predictions of His death, it is very significant that the traditional gospel completely ignores this connection and insists that Jesus' thought of His death was dominated by Isa. liii., which Jesus is recorded to have cited only once, and even then it is in a saying recorded by Luke only (Luke xxii. 37, " And He was reckoned with the transgressors "). Although the writers of the New Testament frequently cite Isa. liii. in reference to the death of Jesus, there can be no doubt whatever that, judging from the record of His sayings it was in His own thought quite secondary to Dan. vii. In comparison with apostolic thought, the sayings of Jesus show a striking absence of reference to Isa. liii. We have only this almost incidental citation in the Lucan passage. Nowhere does Jesus call Himself by the Isaianic term "servant of the Lord." The Danielic term " Son of man " is always on His lips. In none of the more specific predictions of His sufferings as the fulfilment of prophecy does Jesus refer to Isa. liii. but always uses language that refers to the prophecy

of Daniel. The reason for the subsequent change of
emphasis was probably that Isa. liii. offered the Jew
associations with the idea of animal sacrifice,—" He
was led as a lamb to the slaughter." And it supplied
a pretext for thinking of the death of Jesus as substitutionary suffering of the penalty deserved by
men,—" He hath laid on Him the iniquity of us all "
(v. 6).

But the context (Luke xxii. 35–38) makes it clear
that Jesus in citing these words had no idea of substitutionary suffering in His mind. He had just
enjoined upon His disciples a change of conduct.
When He first sent them out to preach, He sent them
" without purse and wallet and shoes," " but now,"
He says, " he that hath a purse let him take it, and
likewise a wallet : and he that hath none let him sell
his cloke and buy a sword." This change of conduct
cannot have been enjoined because of a change in
the spirit and intent of Jesus, which we have every
reason to believe remained constant. It must therefore be explained as due to a change in the attitude
of those to whom His preachers were sent. And
here we know there had been change. When the
Twelve first went out, they had been given adequate
hospitality : they had lacked nothing. But now the
life of Jesus Himself was sought by the heads and
representatives of the nation, of which fact His
words, " And He was reckoned with the transgressors,"
were a simple recognition (cf. Mark xiv. 48, 49, " And
Jesus answered and said unto them, Are ye come out,
as against a robber, with swords and staves to seize
Me ? "). And His followers could expect no better
treatment than He received.

If we thus take the words in their context, we see
that Jesus, when He spoke of Himself as " reckoned
amongst the transgressors," was thinking of the

actual historic conditions of the moment, such as
would call for a modification of His disciples' methods.
Those who reckoned Him with the transgressors were
the high priests and the rest of the Sanhedrin with
Jerusalem and the nation behind them. In the
recorded use of these words, therefore, Jesus is
certainly not thinking that God reckoned Him with
the transgressors, nor is it likely that if He ever
thought of God as doing so, He would have used this
expression to describe the attitude of God's opponents.

(d)

In considering Mark x. 45, " For verily the Son of
man came not to be ministered unto, but to minister,
and to give His life a ransom for many," we have to
note that the authenticity of the latter part of this
saying has been questioned. Luke (xxii. 27) omits
it. His version of that which precedes it differs
from the Marcan account, and there is a still greater
difference in the time and circumstance accorded to
the sayings. And since it is practically certain that
Luke used Mark, we have to infer that Luke preferred
a version from some other source to that of Mark,
and Luke's profession of accuracy (Luke i. 3) and his
general historicity give weight to his preference. On
the other hand, Luke's setting of the incident is in
itself less likely than Mark's. It is difficult to think
that a contention for precedence could follow hard
upon the last supper and the prediction of betrayal.
The allusion to the number of the Twelve in " the
twelve tribes of Israel " (Luke xxii. 30) suggests a
time before the defection of Judas. Mark's earlier
setting is therefore much more probable.

Luke also misses the characteristic double parallelism
of the Marcan version, in which the first and third

and the second and fourth clauses correspond (as, e.g., in Psa. lv. 21) :—

(*a*) Whosoever would become great among you, shall be your minister :

(*b*) And whosoever would be first among you, shall be slave of all.

(*c*) For verily the Son of man came not to be ministered unto, but to minister,

(*d*) And to give His life a ransom for many,

the ministering of (*c*) corresponding to that of (*a*), and the ransoming of (*d*) corresponding to the slavery of (*b*). Both these considerations are in favour of the Marcan version, and therefore of the authenticity of the last clause of Mark x. 45.

It is often assumed that this figure of " ransom " should be understood in the terms of the traditional gospel as speaking of the remission of sins by the death of Jesus. In order to make the figure yield this meaning it must be understood as a ransoming from death or some other penalty. But the commonest meaning of the word, and therefore that which, in the absence of indications to the contrary, has priority of likelihood, is that of enfranchisement from slavery or captivity. And the context and parallelism make it almost certain that it has this meaning here. The whole discourse is of lordship and servitude. The saying that he who would be great among the followers of Jesus must be their servant has its parallel in the saying that the Son of man came not to be served, but to serve : so, too the followers of Jesus must rather be slaves of their brethren than seek to enslave them in the Gentile way (v. 44), for the Son of man came to give His life a ransom for many (v. 45*b*). This sequence indicates that the " ransom " should be understood as ransom

from slavery. If, therefore, we interpret the saying
as ultimately having reference to sin, it tells us that
Jesus looked upon His death as giving man freedom
not from the penalty of sin but from its domination
and tyranny. But it is probably best to take the
words in their widest sense as telling us that Jesus
looked upon His death to make man morally and
spiritually free from all unworthy dominion.

But the saying does not receive its right colouring
until we remember that Jesus is here speaking of
the kingdom of God. The discourse begins with rule
and authority and power, i.e. with kingship. Jesus
speaks of the state of things amongst " the Gentiles,"
and adds, " But it is not so among you." The contrast with the Gentiles suggests that He is speaking
to His hearers as Jews, but as Jews in the ideal, i.e.
as " sons of the kingdom," since, in the actual, Jewish
rulers had domineered and tyrannized. Jesus is
thus contrasting the kingdoms of the Gentiles with
the kingdom of God. This is confirmed by the connected sayings which follow in the Lucan version
and speak expressly of the kingdom (Luke xxii. 29,
30). Jesus, therefore, in Mark x. 43–45 is describing
kingship in the kingdom of God. In this case, by
ransoming He would mean ransoming from unrighteous
servitude into the kingdom of God (as in Tit. ii. 14,
Acts xx. 28, etc.). The death that ransoms men
from false influences must also enthrone God in their
hearts. But if the enthronement of God in the heart
is to come with enfranchisement, it must be voluntary.
Therefore we are led to conclude that Jesus looked for
His death to give men such an idea of God that they
would desire above all things to enthrone Him in
their hearts. The ransom that liberates comes from
a love that must reign.

This interpretation accords with the historic conditions and effect of His death. He gave His life in contest with Pharisee and scribe and priest, whose prestige and authority over the people was the greatest external obstacle to Israel's acceptance of His truth (cf. Matt. xxiii. 13, Mark xii. 1–9). His cleansing of the Temple put the religious authorities in a position in which they must either acknowledge His authority or by killing Him lose their prestige with His followers. And His disciples' freedom from the prestige of the Jerusalem authorities is, according to the early chapters of Acts, one of the most marked of the results of His death. So, too, the apostles' earliest message to Israel was that Jesus the crucified was the anointed king, the Christ. The living centre of their religion was the kingship of Jesus and the experience of the power of God—the actual kingship of God—in their hearts, which came with the acceptance of Jesus' truth. The death of Jesus had ransomed them from wrong domination by establishing God's kingship within them.

(e)

In considering Jesus' utterances about His death we must not overlook those connected with the anointing at Bethany. The woman's action seems to have been misread in different ways by both bystanders and commentators. Her act is probably not to be understood as the provision of a luxury uncommon among the Jews and hardly in keeping with the spirit of Jesus. We should rather see in this anointing the significance, which it so often bears in the Old Testament of a recognition of kingship, the Messiah being specifically " the Anointed." The manner of the act suggests it,—" She brake the cruse and poured " the ointment " over His head " (Mark xiv. 3). Had it been the gift of a luxury, a more economic use would have produced better results. The pouring of ointment upon the head was the method of high priestly and regal designation and consecration (Exod. xxix. 7; Lev. viii. 12; 1 Sam. x. 1; 2 Kings ix. 3, 6). Nor has it been uncommon to break vessels used for especially sacred acts, as though they had become too sacred for common use.

If we may accept this explanation, more point is given to the words by which Jesus defends the act: " For ye have the poor always with you, and whensoever ye will ye can do them good, but Me ye have not always " (Mark xiv. 7). For if the action is regarded merely as the provision of a luxury, the possibility of providing luxury for our friends is as permanent as that of giving charity to the poor, and it would be contrary to the spirit of Jesus to claim any uniqueness or precedence as a recipient of luxury. But in His Messiahship Jesus was unique and as Messiah He did not rank with the rest of humanity. To anoint Him as Messiah in such a way and at such a time was a deed more valuable to the world than much giving of alms.

And it also becomes easier to regard as authentic the saying, " And verily I say unto you, Wheresoever the gospel shall be preached throughout the whole world, that also which this woman hath done shall be spoken of for a memorial of her " (Mark xiv. 9), for it is thus analogous to the exclamation (Matt. xvi. 17) with which Jesus welcomed Peter's confession of His Messiahship. The words are seen to rise directly out of the incident, for the gospel of the nearness of the kingdom of God was the gospel of the Messiahship of Jesus. And the woman's act needs this interpretation in order to justify so great a memorial.

So viewed, the interest of the incident and its connected sayings is great. They tell us that Jesus regarded the gospel He preached as essentially one with the gospel to be preached after His death and as essentially one with the fact of His Messiahship. They also tell us that He regarded His death as in line with the effort of His life.   The gist of His thought lies in the turn He gives to the woman's act. She anointed Him as king : He says, " She hath done what she could : she hath anointed My body afore-hand for the burying " (Mark xiv. 8). He accepts the ascription of kingship but puts into the anointing a deeper truth than the woman intended,—it is through suffering and death that He will reign. And here we have the same sequence of thought as in Mark viii. 29, 31, where the disciples' confession of Jesus' Messiahship is followed immediately by the forecast of sufferings and death.

A consideration in support of this view is that in Mark (xiv. 10, 11) Judas' visit to the high priests follows immediately upon the anointing at Bethany. For there is considerable probability in the opinion of those who hold that the treachery of Judas consisted not only in assisting the arrest of Jesus, but still more in divulging the fatal secret of His Messiahship. This is made likely by the fact that the high priest evidently knew of the claim (Mark xiv. 61) but could not produce the necessary two witnesses and so must endeavour to make the prisoner incriminate Himself. Judas did not believe in Jesus' Messiahship, and whatever may have been his part in the confession of Cæsarea Philippi, the anointing at Bethany must have exasperated him and may well have determined him to leave One who was thus courting destruction. It placed in his hands information which was of value to the authorities and it provided some sort of an excuse for his defection. Jesus, knowing Judas' attitude towards Him, knew what use might be made of such an incident as the anointing, and in view of this we should probably see in His words, " She hath anointed My body aforehand for the burying," an additional element,—the ironic recognition that this act of homage was to prove a factor in His death.

(f)

The words spoken over the bread and wine at the last supper give us the most intimate and direct indication of Jesus' thought of His death. His reference to the covenant defines His meaning as to the cup, but the figure of the broken bread is left without definition. Some have thought that in it He proffers Himself as the paschal lamb, in which case He interprets His death by a comparison with the enfranchisement of Israel from Egypt, a thought similar to the utterance of Mark x. 45, " To give His life a ransom for many." But against this conclusion there are two considerations. Had Jesus intended to be understood so, it would have been more natural and intelligible if He had spoken the words over the paschal lamb itself. Of course, it is not certain that the last supper was the passover : the Fourth Gospel places it on the evening before that on which the passover was eaten, and certain statements of the other Gospels confirm this date. But this only renders the second consideration more cogent : if Jesus in the breaking and giving of the bread intended Himself to be understood as the paschal lamb, He would probably have made some such explicit reference as He did in the giving of the cup, nor would the tradition of such a reference be likely, had it been made, to have been lost.

We should probably, therefore, interpret the figure of the broken bread in the simplest way as food. It is so understood in the great discourse on the bread of life in John vi., which gives a still more definite interpretation, " It is the spirit that quickeneth ; the flesh profiteth nothing : the words that I have spoken unto you are spirit, and are life " (John vi. 63), implying that His death would make a way into the hearts of men for the truth by which He lived and by which they also might live. Modern scholarship does not allow us to regard the discourses of the Fourth Gospel as a verbatim report of Jesus' utterances, but this particular saying (John vi. 63) is little more than an interpretation of Jesus' words over the broken bread by His own earlier use of the same figure,—" Man shall not live by bread alone, but by every word that proceedeth out of the mouth of God " (Matt. iv. 4, Luke iv. 4).

His words in the giving of the bread thus tell us that He looked upon His death as the means to an intimate and quickening fellowship, an internal oneness, between Himself and His followers, i.e. to the effective achievement of all that His intercourse with them had begun and tended to. And whatever else we may see in this fellowship and oneness of Jesus with His followers, the essence of it for our conscious selves must surely be our participation in and appropriation of the truth by which He lived.

This interpretation of the broken bread leads up to Jesus' words over the cup. The bread spoke of a quickening oneness of life between Himself and His followers, which was to be effectively achieved by His complete giving of Himself to them in death : the blood of the covenant speaks of a bond between man and God made effective by the participation of both in one life.

The words, " This is My blood of the covenant," are directly reminiscent of the creative beginning of Hebrew theocracy and show how near Jesus' thought

of His death was to His concern for the establish-
ment of the kingdom of God. That He meant His
words to be so understood appears from those that
follow, " Verily I say unto you, I will no more drink
of the fruit of the vine, until that day when I drink
it new (i.e. of a new kind) in the kingdom of God "
(Mark xiv. 25), implying that He was laying down
His life for the kingdom of God and looked upon His
death as a means to it.

This figure of Jesus' death is based on the primitive
rite of the blood-covenant, which was the cementing
of a binding fellowship through the participation of
the covenanting parties in the life of one victim.
They drank or were smeared or sprinkled with its
blood, and were thus made one with each other by
being made one with it. And when we turn to the
story of the blood of the covenant (Exod. xxiv. 3–8)
we see that the spiritual centre of it was Israel's
promise to obey God (vs. 3 and 7) : it was Israel's
acceptance of God's kingship. So that in this figure
Jesus speaks of His death as that which will make
God's kingship effective, and will therefore establish a
new and now effective covenant.

All four accounts of the supper agree in giving us
Jesus' reference to the blood of the covenant. The
First Gospel alone adds " unto remission of sins "
(Matt. xxvi. 28). But there is reason for regarding
this phrase as an editorial addition. The author of
the First Gospel is in this passage (Matt. xxvi. 26–29)
following Mark (xiv. 22–25), and it is noticeable that
his insertion of the clause in question compels him
to introduce the next sentence with a " but," though
its sequence to what precedes is so close that in Mark
it follows without any conjunction.

Something belonging to the conditions under which
the First Gospel was produced is apparently responsible

for this addition, for Matthew also omits Mark's and Luke's statement that John's preaching and baptism were " unto remission of sins " (cf. Matt. iii. 2 and Mark i. 4, Luke iii. 3). In this obviously connected addition and omission the oldest tradition has evidently been modified in the interests of a later theology which specifically connected the remission of sins with Jesus' death in a way that was incompatible with earlier belief.

Matthew's addition obscures and confuses the figure, for the sin-offering was not a covenant-making sacrifice, and had place and efficacy only within the covenant, and it is impossible to question that it was the covenant sacrifice that Jesus had in mind. And it is important to mark that in this evidently unauthentic phrase we have the only words in which Jesus is reported specifically to have connected His death with the remission of sins.

(g)

The cry from the cross, " My God, My God, why hast Thou forsaken Me ? " has been cited in support of the traditional view that Jesus suffered as a vicarious sacrifice for sinners and that in undergoing their penalty He was for the time actually forsaken by God. But if we thus insist upon this literal interpretation of the words, we have also to acknowledge that they tell us that Jesus did not know why He was forsaken of God and must therefore ask. But to acknowledge that Jesus did not know why He was forsaken of God is quite incompatible with the dogma that He came in order that He might undergo this very experience, a dogma upon which the traditional view depends.

What the words actually do import is less easy to say, because we do not know whether they were followed by more of the Psalm (xxii.) which they begin, or in any case whether they meant to Jesus what they appear to mean to the psalmist. But it must be remembered that here Jesus is citing the words of another and that where He speaks in His own words from the cross He uses the word, "Father," that speaks of unbroken communion with God (Luke xxiii. 34, 46). We have the same term in the prayer of Gethsemane (Mark xiv. 36), and if that prayer is any indication of the mind of Jesus in the hours that followed, it certainly does not indicate or foreshadow a break in His fellowship with God. This is seen not only in the words, " Not what I will, but what Thou wilt," but still more in the figure used, " Remove this cup from Me " (Mark xiv. 36) ; for it is not sufficiently recognized that the cup is not symbolic of suffering only : it has a strong suggestion of fellowship. Jesus had this same evening taken the cup and given it to His disciples as a token of communion in His life poured out, and it is hardly possible that the figure of His prayer should be barren of this significance. It tells us that Jesus did not think of God as thrusting upon Him an unshared sorrow. Yet the fellowship was one from which Jesus could not but shrink, for it was fellowship in God's suffering at His failure to save Israel. If this is so, it determines the meaning of the word "forsaken" as expressing, not an experience of God's displeasure, but a missing of God's help in His sorrow, which could not but be, if His sorrow was God's sorrow (see pp. 236 ff.). And this agrees with the meaning of the word in the Psalm where the emphasis is upon lack of help from God rather than suspicion of displeasure in Him.

We have thus considered all that we can rely on as giving information of what Jesus thought, and would have His followers think, of His death, and everything shows that He looked upon it as vitally connected with His gospel of the kingship of God and as instrumental to its realization. This kingship, as we have seen, depended upon man's knowing and accepting Jesus' truth of God, so that, as far as we can speak of intent and purpose in His death, He died that His truth of God might be the possession of mankind.

CHAPTER III

THE GOSPEL AND THE EARLY CHURCH

(1)

BETWEEN the preaching of Jesus and the vogue of the traditional gospel lie the New Testament writers. And we cannot do justice to the part they played unless we keep certain considerations in mind. For it is claimed that they justify the transition.

We must not forget that the transition is a serious one. If we accept the traditional gospel, we affirm that the death of Jesus was necessary to the forgiveness of sins and in so doing we contradict the teaching of Jesus, for nothing is surer in the record of His life than that He pronounced forgiveness before He began to teach that He must die and that He taught conditions of forgiveness without any reference to His death. Nor does He anywhere speak of His death as necessary for the forgiveness of sins.

Those who maintain that Jesus' death was necessary for the forgiveness of sins sometimes assume that His teaching on forgiveness could not, for that very reason, have the finality of subsequent Christian doctrine. But if this is so, then either Jesus was not aware that His death was necessary to forgiveness, which is quite incompatible with the Christology of those who maintain this necessity, or He knew it but spoke about His death without hinting that it was necessary for the forgiveness of man and taught the way to forgiveness without making any reference to His death The traditional gospel thus implies that

there is a contradiction between the teaching of
Jesus and what it maintains to be the main thing
which He came to do.

And this implied contradiction reappears in the
interpretation which the traditional gospel puts upon
the death of Jesus. Nothing is more variable in
Christian theology than the theories of atonement,
which seek to show why and how the death of Jesus
was a necessary condition to the forgiveness of man.
His death has been explained as a cheating of the
devil, or a ransom paid to the devil, or a satisfaction
of the offended majesty of God, or a substitutionary
suffering of the pangs of hell merited by us, etc. The
one thing common to all these theories is that they
say that the death of Jesus was necessary because of
something quite different from the historic conditions
which the Gospels tell us actually led to it. They all
agree that the real reason of His death was not that
it was the inevitable outcome of Jesus' utter faithfulness to God in face of a hostile world, but that it was
due to the necessity of fulfilling certain divinely
ordained conditions of man's forgiveness. And the
conditions for which they stipulate always involve
the assumption that man could not be forgiven unless
Jesus suffered and died, though the variety and
mutually contradictory nature of the theories proffered
in support of the assumption cannot but reflect on
its validity.

The traditional gospel thus forbids us to see Jesus'
death as the culmination of His life. It makes the
main significance of His death to lie in factors introduced at that point and not operative before. It
assumes that He died to create a gospel essentially
different from the gospel which He lived to preach.
It assumes that the agony of Gethsemane and the
heartbreak of Golgotha were not the full tide of the

sorrow that wept over Jerusalem, but that something new and quite different intervened. It insists that we must not understand the final sufferings of Jesus' spirit as the agony that love suffers when men reject what love would do for them. It claims that we must find the explanation of His final sufferings in the necessity for fulfilling the condition of man's forgiveness.

The attempts that have been made to restate the traditional gospel in terms compatible with the moral sense of the age do not touch the point at issue here. So long as we stipulate that the death of Jesus was a necessary condition to the forgiveness of sins, we contradict Jesus' own teaching as to forgiveness and are precluded from regarding His death as the forthright outcome of His life. We cannot both retain the traditional gospel with its theological stipulations and regard the death of Jesus as one with His life.

The death of Jesus is without doubt the supreme power in bringing men to repentance and in assuring them of God's forgiveness, but the traditional gospel is not a simple recognition and use of this power. Were it so, it would be a true part, though still only a part, of the gospel that Jesus preached. But it insists that apart from the death of Jesus there can be no forgiveness. It thereby belies the relationship between the life of Jesus and His death, and so partly obscures and perverts His power to help mankind.

The whole possibility of forgiveness for man lies in God's love for the unjust and evil, which love was the centre of Jesus' teaching and the ruling passion of His life. And His death, more than all else in His life, assures us of this truth and gives it power over us. We may even say that we should have lost the one thing that makes it finally credible, if Jesus had avoided the cross to which loyalty led Him or had shown Himself unhurt in spirit by His people's rejection of God's truth. In this sense Jesus' death was essential to His gospel, not because it made God able to forgive, but because it made men able to believe in a God whose love is great enough to forgive redemptively,—not because it made a way for men into God's love, but because it drove a way for God's love into the hearts and minds of men.

We have thus to choose between the traditional gospel and the validity of Jesus' own teaching together with the historic intelligibility and spiritual power of His death as seen in relation to His life and teaching.

The obvious retort to this statement will be, How then do the New Testament writings include what warrants, or at least seems to warrant, the traditional gospel? In reply to which we may anticipate the results of this chapter by saying that, in the main, their gospel is much nearer the gospel that Jesus preached than it is to the traditional gospel. Forgiveness of sins is only one element in their gospel and is by no means always connected with the death of Jesus. Their great emphasis upon His death is grounded mainly upon its relation to His life and teaching. But, on the other hand, certain factors of Jewish thought with which they had to take account, and from which all of them were not themselves quite free, sometimes led them to forms of expression that seem to involve the ideas of the traditional gospel. But these factors of Jewish thought are not part of the teaching of Jesus and are mostly antagonistic to it.

(2)

Jesus' figure of the blood-covenant was adopted by New Testament writers in a way which suggests that, when they were not under the influence of some particular stress, it was the normal figure for their thought of His death. But it was almost inevitable that other sacrificial terms should be added. The creative priority and prominence of the covenant sacrifice was bound up with its solitariness in the far past, while sacrifices of other sort were the more than daily ritual of the Temple and could not but have large place in Jewish thought and sentiment.

Prominent among the commoner Jewish sacrifices was the sin-offering, which afforded the Jew a ready and forcible figure for an element of the experience created in him by the death of Jesus. One of the most marked of Christian experiences is in the power of the death of Jesus to move to repentance and to give assurance of forgiveness. This power does not seem to need any other explanation than that by His death Jesus gave final embodiment and seal and penetrative force to the truth for and in which He lived,—that God's love was too great to be annulled by man's sin. If it is said that such an explanation does not do justice to the Christian experience of God's condemnation of sin, let it be remembered that Jesus defines righteousness in the terms of love (Mark xii. 28–31, Matt. xxii. 34–40) and that nothing but love can rightly condemn lovelessness. So understood, the meaning and power of the death of Jesus as related to forgiveness are purely personal, ethical and spiritual, and are seen and felt in most intimate connection with His life and teaching. Indeed, without His life and teaching His death would in this sense be meaningless and powerless. And it is very easy to see that a Jew who found God's forgiving and redemptive love effective in the death of Jesus would readily find a figure for his experience in the sin-offering, not because the method and idea of the sin-offering contained the secret of the power of Jesus' death, but rather the opposite,—because the death of Jesus effected what the sin-offering promised but could not perform (cf. Heb. x. 4). And to speak of the death of Jesus as a sin-offering helped the Jew to pass from the mechanical and unspiritual idea of animal sacrifice to the ethical and spiritual experience of God's forgiveness as known in Jesus. This justified the use of such terms by New Testament writers. Nor are they to blame if subsequent thinkers, less spiritual than they, took what was with them an incident of transition and made of it a theological principle by insisting that the secret of the death of Jesus must be found in those very ideas of animal sacrifice, the insufficiency of which made His work necessary.[1]

We have to remember that when Jewish Christians spoke of the death of Jesus as a sin-offering, they were continuing a process already begun. The Mosaic sin-offering atoned according to the law for very little more than ritual uncleanness and sins of inadvertence; that is, it was not an atonement for sin at all in the more serious sense of the word. For wilful sin no sacrifice was provided in the law. This means that in the earlier stage, with the Jew as with other races, the whole emphasis of the cult was upon its own observance as a special and separate interest of life. Apart from the possibility of mistakes in the cult, the problem of human wrong-doing was outside

---

[1] As an illustration of this, cf. S. Dill, *Roman Society from Nero to Marcus Aurelius*, p. 555 : " The greatest and most impressive rite in the worship of Cybele was the taurobolium. There was none which so excited the suspicion and indignation of the Christian apologists, from Tertullian to Prudentius, because in its ceremony of the cleansing blood, and in its supposed effects in moral regeneration and remission of sins, it seemed invented by the ingenuity of dæmons to be a travesty of the sacrifice on Calvary."

its scope. But with the moral and spiritual development of the race many found it intolerable that the supreme interest of the divinely ordained cult should stand quite apart from the most serious interest of life. This situation could be met only in two ways :—

(*a*) The sin-offering could come to be regarded as atoning for wilful sin as well as for ritual offences.

(*b*) The importance, and even the divine origin, of the whole cult of sacrifice could be questioned and the supreme emphasis put upon moral and spiritual conditions. This attitude is found in Psa. xl. 6 ff., Isa. i. 11 ff., Jer. vii. 22 ff.

The second attitude became more and more difficult as Judaism became the religion of a book, but there is reason to conclude that it represents the mind of Jesus. He questioned the divineness of the Mosaic law on more than one point (Mark vii. 14 ff., x. 5 ff.).[1] And His whole spirit is embodied in the citation attributed to Him, " I desire mercy and not sacrifice " (Matt. xii. 7). But a belief in the literal inspiration of the law seems to have been very general amongst the Jews of that time. This confined them to the first alternative (*a*) : they regarded the sin-offering as atoning for sin in a far wider sense than the law specified. The sin-offering thus represented a very important interest in their religion, and they naturally sought a place for it in their following of Jesus. The obvious solution of their quest was to regard the death of the Messiah as a sin-offering, to look on the Mosaic ritual as prophetic of the sacrifice of the Messiah and to search the Scriptures for anything that could be construed into a prophecy of the Messiah's death as sin-offering. The recognition of some such process of thought as this is necessary to explain how it came to be (as Dr. Rashdall asserts,

[1] See page 195.

Idea of Atonement, pp. 78 ff.) that the idea of Jesus' death as atonement was in the first instance accepted on authority from Old Testament prophecy.

There were, however, other important factors in the thought of their time which led the thinkers of the New Testament to put great emphasis upon this figure of the sin-offering as applied to the death of Jesus.

We may first reckon with the difficulty which the Jews had in accepting a crucified Messiah. To us it is Christ crucified that shows most indubitably divine, so different is our thought from theirs. This difficulty imposed upon Jesus' followers the need for explaining His death in a way that would satisfy the Jew. Thus an artificial element was added to the intrinsic importance of His death. Now the Jews' difficulty in accepting a crucified Messiah depended chiefly upon their conviction that calamity, and especially early and violent death, proved God's displeasure with the sufferer and showed that the sufferer had sinned. This doctrine was not part of Jesus' teaching : in Luke xiii. 1–5 we are told that others quoted it to Him and that He answered, " I tell you nay." But it was apparently very popular [1] (see John ix. 2), so that a Jew found great difficulty in thinking that the Messiah could suffer crucifixion, such an end being especial evidence of the curse of God (Deut. xxi. 23). " Christ crucified " was thus " to the Jews a stumbling-block."

The first endeavour to meet this difficulty was to deny its premise by proving from the scriptures that " it behove the Messiah to suffer." This was in the

[1] The converse of this idea, to the effect that prosperity was evidence of God's favour, may be seen in the astonishment with which the disciples received Jesus' words, " How hardly shall they that have riches enter into the kingdom of God " (Mark x. 23–26).

line of Jesus' own thought, that a true service of
God would involve suffering. "It cannot be that a
prophet perish out of Jerusalem" (Luke xiii. 33;
cf. Acts vii. 51, 52). But since the suffering and
death of Jesus were incurred in the service of others
and by the sin of others, it was very easy to pass
from this earlier position, which denied the commonly
accepted theory that all suffering resulted from sin
committed, to one that accepted it but explained
that Jesus suffered for the sins of others.

But the statement that Jesus suffered for the sins
of others is capable of two very different interpretations. A father suffers for his son's sins in proportion as he loves him. But in primitive conditions, if
a criminal cannot be caught the primitive sense of
justice and the primitive idea of divine demands are
satisfied by killing one of his family or fellow-tribes-
men. Here we have two ways in which a man may
suffer for the sins of his fellows, one of which is to us
a spiritual power and the other an interesting example
of primitive ideas upon which it would now be immoral
to act. So that when it is said that Jesus died for
the sins of others we need to ask further which of these
two meanings is to be taken.

We have already seen that it was natural for the
Jewish followers of Jesus to think of His death under
the figure of sin-offering, and it is easy to see how
this figure would influence their answer to the difficulty of a crucified Messiah. It would suggest that
His suffering and death for others was suffering and
death as sin-offering. What was first a helpful poetic
figure is converted into an unethical interpretation of
Jesus' death in order to make terms with an unethical
idea of God's providence. For it is quite clear that
when an animal victim is thought of as dying for the
sins of man, the transaction bears the nature of the

second rather than the first of the two instances given above. It involves the primitive, unethical ideas which preceded the development of personality.

Nor does it mend matters to say that the sin-offering was a gift to appease God or a fine demanded by Him, for the transaction is still mechanical and not spiritual. And if it is said that the animal sacrifice had spiritual value as a confession of what man deserved, we cannot but ask why the confession without the sacrifice would not have served better, for surely it does not accentuate my sense of responsibility to make something else suffer for my wrong-doing. Or it may be said that the animal sacrifice was the imperfect expression of a need ultimately satisfied by the perfect sacrifice of Jesus. But if so, then what makes the sacrifice of Jesus perfect is the entry of moral and spiritual elements impossible in the animal. It is therefore by these elements that we must interpret the perfect sacrifice. This means that to call the death of Jesus a sacrifice gives a new meaning to the word " sacrifice " but does not explain the death of Jesus.

The possibility of confusion of thought on this point was increased for the Jew because, despite the above-noted protests of Jeremiah and others, he was convinced that animal sacrifice was a divinely ordained institution.

Connected with the Jews' difficulty in accepting a crucified Messiah was the concomitant one of understanding how it could be that the Messiah should be rejected by the chosen people. The difficulty was accentuated by the belief in predestination, the assumption being that whatever happened had been ordained by God. God, they therefore argued, must have ordained that the Jews should reject and kill Jesus. " They stumbled at the word, being disobedient ; whereunto they were ordained " (1 Pet. ii. 8) : " God gave them a spirit of stupor, eyes that they should not see " (Rom. xi. 8). But if this was so, then God must have had some specific purpose in wanting the Jews to kill Jesus, and therefore the explanation of Jesus' death would not lie in the historic conditions recounted in the Gospel, but in some purpose in God's mind that moved Him to ordain the transaction of that history. The question then arose, Why did God want Jesus to be killed ? And the ritual sacrifice that had already suggested a way out of the first difficulty was made to provide one for this also,—it was necessary that Jesus should suffer as a sacrifice for sin.

To us, as we read the Gospels, the rejection of Jesus by the Jews is no enigma. We see the choice that Jesus put before them in the hope that they would choose the higher and therefore in the confidence that they could choose it, and we see that they shrank from the cost of the higher and chose the lower.

We see, too, that Jesus did not share the idea of predestination which subsequently prevented a simple understanding of His death. It is true that in Mark iv. 11, 12 (Matt. xiii. 13–15, Luke viii. 10) He is recorded to have said to His disciples, " Unto you is given the mystery of the kingdom of God : but unto them that are without, all things are done in parables : that seeing they may see, and not perceive ; and hearing they may hear, and not understand ; lest haply they should turn again and it should be forgiven them." In the position in which this saying is placed it tells us that Jesus spoke in parables in order that He should not be understood, lest, understanding, the people should repent ; but we cannot think that Jesus, who called the people to repent, did not do all possible to aid repentance.

And the reason why the passage was so placed as to have this meaning is not far to seek. Granted the idea that God predetermined that Israel should reject and kill Jesus, it was logical to think that Jesus should co-operate with God in this by withholding anything that might conduce to Israel's repentance. What the saying means when removed from its present context is perhaps idle to speculate, since the compiler who placed it there may have modified it in editing or translating. But if we may take the ἵνα in its not infrequent use as giving result rather than intention, and if we note that " to them that are without all things *happen* " not " are spoken " " in parables," the sense seems to be that they see only the surface of things, like one who hears a parable but does not perceive its meaning, so that seeing they see not.[1] The saying is thus another statement of the charge of Luke xii. 56, " Ye know how to interpret the face of the earth and the heaven : but how is it that ye know not how to interpret this time ? " In any case a saying of such doubtful meaning cannot be set against Jesus' demand for His people's repentance. We cannot but suppose that He believed in the possibility and hoped for the fulfilment of that which He demanded. The words He puts into the mouth of the lord of the vineyard, " They will reverence my son " (Mark xii. 6) suggest that He knew that God shared His hope. His upbraiding of " the cities wherein most of His mighty works were done " (Matt. xi. 20-24, Luke x. 12-15) are not the words of one who conceived of their unrepentance as ordained of God. " Now are they hid from thine eyes " (Luke xix. 42) implies that there was a time when there was no insurmountable bar to Jerusalem's salvation. In the parable of the tares,—" An enemy

[1] Cf. W. C. Allen, *The Gospel According to Saint Mark*, pp. 79, 80.

hath done this " (Matt. xiii. 24 ff.),—Jesus specifically repudiates the idea that God puts evil into the hearts of men, and in the saying, " It is not the will of your Father that one of these little ones should perish " (Matt. xviii. 14) Jesus expressly denies that man's rejection of good can be attributed to the will of God.

To recapitulate : men who believed that God foreordained that Israel should reject and kill Jesus were bound to ask, Why did God want Jesus killed ? And the most obvious answer was an explanation of His death in the terms of animal sacrifice as a sin-offering. But we have seen both that this explanation rests upon ideas that are antagonistic to the spirit of Jesus and that He denied that God predetermines man to evil. He thus cut the ground from the whole process of thought that suggested such an explanation.

Another point of difference between the gospel that Jesus preached and the gospel of the New Testament writers is their emphasis upon His resurrection as the miracle by which God set His seal to the Messiahship of Jesus (see pp. 79, 86, 195f). It has not this significance for us : if to-day a man believes that Jesus was the Christ and that God was uniquely in Him, his belief is not grounded upon the apostolic testimony as to a miraculous resurrection, but rather upon what he sees and feels of the moral and spiritual supremacy and power of Jesus in life and death. But it is fairly clear that the apostolic insistence upon the miraculous resurrection of Jesus was another result of the Jewish difficulty of accepting a crucified Messiah : both to the apostles and their converts the resurrection was evidence that, despite such a death, God set His seal to the Messiahship of Jesus. But it can hardly be questioned that in making this use of the resurrection to combat a Jewish prejudice, they were making the sort of appeal to " signs " which Jesus condemned (Mark viii. 12).[1] It must also be noted that the tendency to emphasize the resurrection was probably strengthened later by the Gentile desire for assurance as to the future life, an assurance which the Jew already possessed.

(3)

In considering the gospel of the New Testament writers we also need to remind ourselves that Hebrew speech was far more figurative and Hebrew thinking far less systematic than those of Western Europe. We do not find them reasoning with defined terms It is more than questionable whether any of them deliberately attempts to systematize or theologize.

To interpret a figure as though it was a definition is always dangerous and is especially so in the case of Jewish writers. In the New Testament Jesus' death is spoken of in such terms as " ransom," " purchase," " sacrifice," " redemption," " reconciliation," " propitiation," and each of these terms illustrates effec-

---

[1] The statement of Mark viii. 12 is quite clear on this point, but against it two sayings are sometimes quoted :—

(1) " An evil and adulterous generation seeketh after a sign ; and there shall no sign be given unto it, but the sign of Jonah " (Matt. xvi. 4, xii. 39 ; Luke xi. 29). In view of Matt. xii. 40 (which, however, many scholars consider to be a gloss), it is sometimes claimed that we have here a direct appeal to the resurrection as a " sign." But if the Jews were to be given precisely the sort of sign they sought, why were they evil for seeking it ? (Cf. also Luke xvi. 31 for the uselessness of such a sign.) The explanation of Luke xi. 30 is therefore probably correct,—the sign was a messenger with a message from God.

(2) Jesus' reply to the messengers from John (Matt. xi. 4, 5, Luke vii. 22). But it is probable that the cures spoken of here were intended to be understood as figurative of spiritual benefits. For they culminate in, " And the poor have good tidings preached to them." And the concluding words, " And blessed is he, whosoever shall find none occasion of stumbling in Me," would be necessary if the healings were of the soul, but would be quite meaningless after a number of stupendous miracles.

tively an aspect of it : " ransom " speaks of freedom won at great cost : " purchase " reminds those for whom Jesus died that they are not their own : " redemption " speaks of costly restoration to rightful lordship, etc. But if we try to press from these figures a meaning or reason for the death of Jesus other than that suggested by the gospel history we shall find that we get discordant meanings from the various terms—as, for instance, from " propitiation " and " ransom." If Jesus in His death was a propitiation set forth by God (Rom. iii. 25), His death cannot be regarded as a ransom paid to God. But if not to God, then to whom ? And the question shows us that these figures, beautiful and powerful as they are in calling thought to various aspects of Jesus' death, become difficult and contradictory when we insist on seeing in them the pronouncements of theology.

A special occasion for caution is found in the occurrence, particularly in the epistles of Paul and the Epistle to the Hebrews, of figurative argument used in a way quite foreign to our thought and rather quaint than illuminating. Thus Paul writes, " Now this Hagar is mount Sinai in Arabia, and answereth to the Jerusalem that now is " (Gal. iv. 25 ; cf. Heb. vii. 1–10). It is clear that one may do the thought of such writers great wrong by taking a figure literally or by seeing an interpretative analogy in what is only a poetic association. Without special reason we have no right to assume that words like, " Our passover hath been sacrificed for us, even Christ " (1 Cor. v. 7), are less figurative than words like, " The rock was Christ " (1 Cor. x. 4).

(4) THE PAULINE EPISTLES.

In considering what the gospel meant to the first followers of Jesus, Paul's epistles are of greatest importance not only because they are our earliest documents, but because Paul is especially claimed as an authority by the adherents of the traditional gospel.

For the purpose in hand it is not necessary to discuss the authenticity of the Pauline epistles. Many modern scholars look upon the epistles to the Romans, Corinthians, Thessalonians, Galatians and Philippians as of more undoubted authenticity than those to Timothy and Titus and even than those to the Colossians and Ephesians. But in so far as we may find reason to doubt that any parts of these letters were from Paul's hand, they are at least good evidence for the thought of those with whom his influence was dominant ; so that the question of authenticity would arise here only in case of considerable discrepancy of thought between those epistles that are universally admitted to be genuine and those that have been challenged.

(a)

It cannot be denied that Paul, when he writes of the death of Jesus in terms of animal sacrifice and especially when he connects such terms with the idea of justification, does use expressions that can be cited in support of the traditional gospel and of the theology behind it ; but he also uses expressions such as, " I have been crucified with Christ " (Gal. ii. 20), which seem to imply a different understanding of Jesus' death. The extreme difficulty of making such differing expressions harmonize with each other suggests that they represent sides of Paul's thinking which he himself had never brought into unity with each other. And other considerations make this probable.

It is clear in the first place that Paul left no definite and completely elaborated theory of the atonement, otherwise subsequent theology would hardly have been able to appeal to him with such diversity of result. Then we know that Paul shared with the Jews of his day certain ideas which, as we have seen, were not held by Jesus and which could not form an integral part of any system of thought based upon His teaching. The Rabbinic training of Paul doubtless accentuated this element of his thought, especially with regard to the directly divine origin of the law. And it is worthy of note that the traditional gospel appeals mainly to the only New Testament writer who had had Rabbinic training and to those passages of his writings in which his mind seems least free from what he brought with him into the service of Christ.

The energy of Paul's thought brings into prominence discrepancies that were latent in others, and we find in his writings expressions which suggest two mutually incompatible ideas of the death of Jesus. One of these is closely connected with certain Jewish tenets which were repudiated by Jesus and looks upon the death of Jesus as a substitutionary sacrifice, thus approximating to the traditional gospel in its statement that the death of Jesus was a necessary preliminary to forgiveness and therefore contradicting Jesus' teaching as to forgiveness. The other is free from elements foreign to the thought of Jesus and centres round the Christian's fellowship with Jesus in His death.

When we ask which of these ideas was most intimate to Paul's experience of Jesus, there can be little doubt. When he is most deeply moved he always speaks in terms of fellowship with Christ. He uses expressions which might mean that Christ died as our substitute or representative and then, when he comes to vital application, he argues as though they were to be understood in the terms of fellowship (cf., e.g., Rom. vi. 1–6 as following iii. 25). It almost seems as though in Paul's thought the idea of Jesus' death as propitiation and substitution served chiefly as an antidote to the non-Christian elements in his belief, so that to a large extent they cancelled each other out and left his inmost experience of Christ free from elements foreign to the teaching of Christ. Paul's own words suggest as much, for one of the great interests of his doctrines of justification and propitiation was the attainment of freedom from the law.

These considerations must be borne in mind when we are reading what Paul wrote to Jews, either as converts or opponents, for " To the Jews I became as a Jew, that I might gain Jews " (1 Cor. ix. 20). In dealing with them the necessities of the case would naturally lead him to emphasize that part of his thought which dealt with and met the difficulties arising from the non-Christian elements of Jewish thought which he shared. And it must be remembered that in argument there is always an incentive to accept everything in our opponents' tenets that can be turned against them on the particular point at issue, and that this incentive is strong in proportion to the urgency of the issue.

This caution is especially relevant to certain passages on which great stress is laid by those who claim that the traditional gospel is Paul's gospel, i.e. Rom. iii. 25, 26, and v. 9, where the blood of Jesus is spoken of as the means to justification. If this is an adequate expression of Paul's experience, and if it means that the death of Jesus was a necessary preliminary and condition to the forgiveness of man, then, as we have seen, it contradicts Jesus' teaching on forgiveness, and we have to choose between the Apostle and his Master. But we must remember

5

that the whole argument of the earlier chapters of the Epistle to the Romans turns upon the idea of justification, in connection with which the following facts are to be noted :—

(1) Jesus Himself makes no use of the term in the Pauline sense. When He said that the publican " went down to his house justified rather than " the Pharisee (Luke xviii. 14), He evidently meant that, of the two, the publican was actually more nearly right with God. The same natural meaning is in " by thy words thou shalt be justified and by thy words thou shalt be condemned " (Matt. xii. 37). The idea of justification, in so far as it involves God's regarding the sinner as other than he is, is foreign to the thought of Jesus. His saying, " When ye shall have done all things that are commanded you, say, We are unprofitable servants ; we have done that which it was our duty to do " (Luke xvii. 10), dispenses with the need for the term " justification." The word itself seems inapplicable to Jesus' idea of forgiveness, for to be justified is to regard the gift of forgiveness as a right.

(2) Paul's experience of conversion was not that of finding justification through the death of Jesus, but rather that of accepting Jesus as Christ and Lord. This is the gist of the several accounts of the vision on the road to Damascus, none of which contains any reference to justification. Nor was Paul conscious of any need of it when the vision came upon him : rather he was too sure of his rectitude. Every indication of the extremely good evidence we have is that Paul's sense of sin came after and not before his conversion. On the road to Damascus, when he was " breathing threatening and slaughter against the disciples of the Lord " (Acts ix. 1), he was acting from a sense of duty,—" I verily thought with myself,

that I ought to do many things contrary to the name of Jesus of Nazareth " (Acts xxvi. 9). And his own letter confirms the account of Acts,—he was " as touching the righteousness which is in the law, found blameless " (Phil. iii. 6 ; see also p. 117), which assertion incidentally contradicts the assumption on which his whole argument for justification is based,— that every Jew stood condemned before the law (Rom. iii. 9–20). This contradiction is very significant because there can be little doubt that in the Philippian passage we have a more intimate account of the experience of Paul than in the Roman one. Phil. iii. 6–9 assumes that the law, even when fulfilled, is immeasurably inferior to " the excellency of the knowledge of Christ Jesus my Lord " : the argument of Romans is that " the law is holy, and the command- ment holy, and righteous, and good " (vii. 12), in fact too good for human obedience, " in that it was weak through the flesh," and that Jesus died " that the ordinance of the law might be fulfilled in us " (viii. 3, 4). Romans assumes an absoluteness of authority in the law which is denied by implication in Philippians. This suggests that in Romans Paul is shaping his argument on the assumption that the law has an authority equal to that of the teaching of Jesus. And it is probable that here we have the key to his use of the word " justification."

(3) For it is clear that " justification " is strictly a legal term and begins to lose its significance as soon as it is removed from legal environment. Rom. ii. makes it clear that Paul was writing at the Jews (or Jewish Christians) who sought to be justified by " the works of the law." They evidently sought to fulfil the demands of the law so as to satisfy the Judge and stand acquitted before Him, and apparently they claimed that this was the way to justification.

And whether they were right or wrong, their use of the word in this connection was natural and appropriate. Paul wants to lift the whole idea of God's way with man to another level, where human merit is lost in the abounding goodness of God, but he still calls this higher relationship by the term appropriate to the lower. Now a judicial acquittal is " justification," but to call a Father's forgiveness " justification " is both inadequate and misleading. When Paul came to the conclusion, " By the works of the law shall no flesh be justified," he had logically done with " justification." But to have dropped the word would have made it less easy for legally minded Jews to follow him and possibly less easy for him to explain his position to himself. He therefore captured the legal term to serve the purposes of grace, and in so doing gave the statement of one thing in the terms of its antithesis. And it is to be noted that when in this connection Paul comes to speak more closely of the death of Jesus he does so in the terms of the legal animal sacrifice in order that he may bring it into range with the legal term " justification."

(4) The suggestion that the idea of justification was, so far as Paul himself was concerned, the result, or rather the reaction, of his surviving rabbinism, and was used by him rather because of its polemic and apologetic value than because it was cognate to his own Christian experience, is confirmed by its infrequency apart from his anti-judaistic controversy. Outside the letters to the Romans and Galatians we find the term only in 1 Cor. vi. 11 and Tit. iii. 7, and in neither case is it connected with the death of Jesus. Nor is it easy to say exactly what Paul meant by justification. He does not mean that we thereby escape God's judgment upon our deeds, which, he tells us, we must all abide

(Rom. ii. 6, xiv. 11, 12 ; 2 Cor. v. 10) ; and in confirmation of this we find that his gospel is not merely
something to be believed but something to be obeyed
(Rom. i. 5 ; 2 Thess. i. 8).   To be justified is not, in
Paul's thought, the same thing as to be saved,—
" Much more then, being now justified by His blood,
shall we be saved from the wrath through Him.   For
if, while we were enemies, we were reconciled to God
through the death of His Son, much more, being
reconciled, shall we be saved by His life " (Rom. v.
9, 10).   And if we accept the reading of Rom. v. 1
adopted by the Revisers, " Being therefore justified
by faith, let us have peace with God through our
Lord Jesus Christ," even peace with God is something
other than justification and is not necessarily involved
in it.

It is, then, in connection with this idea of justification that we find the passages in which Paul gives
apparent support to the idea of the death of Jesus
embodied in the traditional gospel.   " All have sinned
and fall short of the glory of God ; being justified
freely by His grace through the redemption that is
in Christ Jesus : whom God set forth to be a propitiation, through faith, by His blood, to shew His
righteousness, because of the passing over of the sins
done aforetime, in the forbearance of God ; for the
showing of His righteousness at this present season :
that He might Himself be just and the justifier of
him that hath faith in Jesus " (Rom. iii. 23–26).   It
is obvious here how the legal idea of justification
tangles Christian thought.   Can we imagine Jesus
teaching that the righteousness of God was likely to
be compromised when He forgave the repentant
sinner ?   In neither of His parables of God's forgiveness (Matt. xviii. 23 ff., Luke vii. 41 f.) is there any
hint that a " propitiation " is necessary in order to

save justice from being compromised by free forgiveness. The gist of both parables would be quite altered by the introduction of any such idea. But when we substitute the legal term " justification " for the personal one " forgiveness " and have to explain how an unjust man can be " justified " (or " accounted just ") otherwise than by being made just, we find ourselves compelled to introduce some such idea as that of substitutionary sacrifice.

The idea of Jesus' death as a propitiation needful for man's justification involves Paul's thought in difficulties. Having just written that God could not justify the sinner without the propitiation in Jesus' blood, he proceeds to tell how Abraham was justified by faith in God apart from any propitiation (Rom. iii. 23–iv. 3 ; cf. Gal. iii. 6). And a little farther on (Rom. iv. 25) justification is made to depend upon the resurrection rather than the death of Jesus, " who was delivered up for our trespasses, and was raised for our justification." We find Paul also committing himself to the rabbinic proposition that " he that hath died is justified from sin " (Rom. vi. 7).

Elsewhere in Paul's writings we find thoughts incompatible with the idea of justification by a propitiatory sacrifice, as the injunction, " Forgive each other, even as God also in Christ forgave you " (Eph. iv. 32 ; cf. Col. iii. 13). Here, as in the teaching of Jesus, it is assumed that God's forgiveness of man is to be the pattern of man's forgiveness of his brother. A propitiatory sacrifice is no more needful for the one than for the other. And in this connection it is interesting to note that twice in the Epistle to the Ephesians we have what are probably sacrificial figures immediately translated into personal terms. In Eph. i. 7, " In whom we have our redemption through His blood " is immediately followed and explained by " the forgiveness of our trespasses, according to the riches of His grace " (cf. Col. i. 14) ; and in ii. 16 Paul, using probably the figure of the sacrifice by which treaties of peace were customarily ratified, speaks of Christ as reconciling Jew and Gentile " in one body unto God through the cross," which he translates for us in v. 18, " For through Him we both have our access in one spirit unto the Father."

In Paul's thinking the idea of Jesus' death as a propitiation was an essential part of his doctrine of justification by faith. When we ask why he should have put such emphasis upon a doctrine which is so unlike the teaching of Jesus, the answer is readily found in a different attitude towards the law. There can be no doubt that the attitude of Jesus towards the law was very much freer than that of Paul. The belief that the law was dictated by God (or given by angels) involved the conviction that it was perfect as far as it went, i.e. in all respects a perfectly true, if not a complete, revelation of God and of His way with men. This conception compelled Paul to seek for a logical bridge from the law to Jesus, i.e. from the less complete to the more complete. But when we are thinking of a matter such as God and His ways with men, if our thought is incomplete it is of necessity also partly inconsistent. And it is impossible to pass by logical steps from the partly inconsistent to the greater truth. Paul, therefore, was attempting the impossible, and the attempt brings him to such strange assertions as that " the law came in besides, that the trespass might abound " (Rom. v. 20), or " I had not known sin except through the law " (Rom. vii. 7) and " apart from the law sin is dead " (Rom. vii. 8) ; the last two assertions being in contradiction to his earlier statement that " As many as have sinned without law shall also perish without law " (Rom. ii. 12).

In this connection we have to remember that a vital element in Paul's gospel was his apostleship to the Gentiles. And his doctrine of justification by faith and not by the works of the law was his method of meeting those who, sharing his belief in the direct divine origin of the law, demanded its observance by Gentile Christians. He saw that to require this would frustrate the work of Christ amongst the Gentiles, and hence his insistence upon the doctrine by which he repudiated the demand (*vide* Rashdall, *The Idea of Atonement*, pp. 104, 105).

But it is questionable whether Paul's idea of the directly divine origin of the law was not rather a conventional axiom than a conviction. For elsewhere he acknowledges that the truth in Jesus not only added to but in part at least superseded and corrected the law as a revelation of God's way with men. We see this even in the controversy as to the Gentiles and the law. It appears in such descriptions as, " The law of the Spirit of life in Christ Jesus made me free from the law of sin and of death " (Rom. viii. 2) and in Paul's frequent asseveration that Christ was to be the final judge of men (2 Thess. i. 8, Rom. ii. 16, 2 Cor. v. 10, 2 Tim. iv. 1, Acts xvii. 31), which was but another way of expressing the moral finality of the teaching of Jesus. And in Col. ii. 14 we have a vivid picture of Jesus' supersession of the law,—for Christ, we are told, has " blotted out the bond written in the ordinances that was against us, which was contrary to us : and He hath taken it out of the way, nailing it to the cross," where " the bond written in the ordinances " can be nothing but the law.

The idea of the death of Jesus as a propitiation is thus dependent upon the doctrine of justification by

faith, which is itself dependent upon the belief in
the directly divine origin of the law. But the point
at which the idea of propitiation appears is extremely
interesting. Paul tells us (Rom. iii. 23–26) that the
death of Jesus as a propitiation was necessary lest
God, in forgiving men, should be thought to deal
lightly with sin. God must do something to show
His antagonism to the sin He forgives (or " passes
over," i.e. does not punish). Now Jesus did not
punish sin, yet no man looking upon His life, and
especially upon His death, could doubt His antagonism
to it. His " sorrow unto death " was a reaction
against sin more impressive and effective than any
infliction of punishment : so Paul, in Rom. viii. 3,
says that in the condemnation of sin the death of
Jesus was more effective than the law. And when
Paul says that " God was in Christ reconciling the
world unto Himself," he implies that God suffered in
the suffering of Jesus. And if, in the death of Jesus,
we know that sin causes suffering to God, then we
have that which evinces God's antagonism to sin
more indubitably and powerfully than any penalty.
But Paul seems to have shrunk from saying explicitly
that God suffered in Christ. Possibly he felt that
such a statement might be a difficulty to his readers.
In any case the thought that God suffers for human
sin is quite outside the juridical range of ideas to
which " justification " belongs. He therefore uses
terms easier to his readers, and possibly to himself,
and instead of saying that God suffered in the suffering
of Jesus, he says that God " set forth Jesus to be a
propitiation . . . by His blood," which seems to be
much the same thing couched in sacrificial language.
But unfortunately the association of this sacrificial
figure with the juridical idea of justification may suggest that it should be interpreted rather in the terms

of substitutionary penalty than in those of suffering love.

(b)

Those who claim the support of Paul for the traditional gospel appeal also to such statements as, " Him who knew no sin He made to be sin on our behalf ; that we might become the righteousness of God in Him " (2 Cor. v. 21), and " Christ redeemed us from the curse of the law, having become a curse for us : for it is written, Cursed is every one that hangeth on a tree " (Gal. iii. 13). But if these words are taken to interpret the death of Jesus as the vicarious suffering of the sinner's state and penalty, the full intake of the plea must not be shirked. For so taken they compel us to think that Paul means that God regarded Jesus in the hours of His agony as the abominable and accursed thing that sin always is in His eyes. This we cannot think.

And, at least in the Corinthian passage, it is quite clear that this was not Paul's thought, for he has just written that " God was in Christ reconciling the world unto Himself " (2 Cor. v. 19). We are therefore compelled to understand the words, " Him who knew no sin He made to be sin on our behalf," rather as meaning that for our sakes, by the suffering of Jesus, sin was shown in its true light.

The context of Gal. iii. 13 indicates fairly clearly what Paul means by saying that Christ " became a curse for us " : he tells us it is because " it is written, Cursed is every one that hangeth on a tree," by which he defines the " curse " to be the experience of crucifixion itself, i.e. it is because Jesus underwent that experience that Paul finds scriptural warrant for saying that He became a curse. So that, in accordance with the thought of the time, the curse, having been verbally fulfilled, might be considered to have spent itself and to be no longer operative. But in saying that " Christ redeemed us from the curse of the law, having become a curse for us," Paul evidently does not mean that God cursed Him instead of us, for then his reason for saying that Jesus " became a curse " would not have been, as he says it was, the fact that He was crucified, but the notion that He was taking the place of the accursed. Paul here does lip-homage to primitive ideas, but at the heart of his argument lies the fact that Jesus underwent an experience so miserable that the law had seen in it the curse of God, but so underwent it as to make it clear that " God was in " Him in that very experience, and therefore that the law's curse was obsolete.

(c)

In Paul's most emphatic and explicit utterances his gospel is found to be one with the gospel that Jesus preached. The tersest statement of it is that " therein is revealed a righteousness of God by faith unto faith " (Rom. i. 17), where the immediately preceding " power of God " and the immediately following and contrasted " wrath of God " (v. 18) make it clear that by " righteousness of God " Paul does not mean a righteousness of man approved of God but the essential goodness of God Himself. That this is his meaning is confirmed by the more elaborate paraphrase of his gospel in Tit. iii. 4 : " But when the kindness of God our Saviour, and His love toward man appeared . . ." Paul's gospel is thus the truth about God's character made known and credible by Jesus and so becoming a saving power in the hearts of all who accept it. For the righteousness of God thus revealed in Jesus invades the hearts of those who accept the revelation : it is " the righteousness of God through faith in Jesus Christ unto all them that believe " (Rom. iii. 22). The human condition, faith, is the witness and the means of the divine invasiveness,—" for this cause it is of faith, that it may be according to grace " (Rom. iv. 16). Man's true righteousness is thus, with Paul, not something of his own initiative, but a reflection and response to God's righteousness, a living belief in His goodness, an honest acknowledgment of God's love : it is " that which is of God by faith " (Phil. iii. 9) : " we all, with unveiled face " (" the veil is done away in Christ "), " reflecting as a mirror the glory of the Lord, are transformed into the same image from glory to glory " (2 Cor. iii. 14, 18). God's glory is the invasive outgoing of His goodness, and that in itself is " the gospel of the glory of the blessed God " (1 Tim. i. 11).

It is very significant of the thought of Paul and other New Testament writers on this matter, and of the Church's abandonment of their point of view, that whereas in the later language of the Church " our Saviour " means Jesus, and Jesus only, the New Testament writers speak of God as " our Saviour " (Luke i. 47; 1 Tim. i. 1, ii. 3, iv. 10, etc.), and when they use the term for Jesus they never take it for granted that He has exclusive right to it, but add His name in all the sixteen instances of its application to Him.

Beside Paul's statement of his gospel in Rom. i. 17 we may place the very emphatic utterance of Galatians. Paul solemnly curses anyone who preaches another gospel than his (Gal. i. 9) : he goes on to say that this gospel was not taught to him by man but was " through revelation of Jesus Christ." He then relates the occasion of this revelation, which proves to be that of which we have three accounts in Acts (ix. 3–9, xxii. 6–11, xxvi. 12–18), the general historicity of which is confirmed by what he says here. According to the accounts of Acts, the revelation that then came was that Jesus was Lord and was one with His followers whom Paul had persecuted : here (Gal. i. 16) it is more briefly put as " the revelation of His Son in me." To this we must add the command to carry the gospel to the Gentiles, which, whether it came with the vision (Acts xxvi. 17), or through Ananias (Acts ix. 15), or upon a subsequent occasion (Acts xxii. 21) was an element of the revelation upon which Paul laid great stress (Gal. i. and ii., Eph. iii. 1–6).

The content, then, of the gospel which Paul claimed to have been revealed to him was that this Jesus whose love made Him so one with His followers that in persecuting them Paul was persecuting Him, this Jesus who had died upon the cross in loyalty to the love of God and the service of man, was Lord and Christ and Son of God. So we read that after his conversion Paul " straightway in the synagogues proclaimed Jesus, that He is the Son of God . . . proving that this is the Christ " (Acts ix. 20–22).

Paul thus (Gal. i. 11–17) specifically identifies his gospel with what came to him by revelation and describes that revelation in such a way as to identify it with that of the vision thrice related in Acts. The revelation contains no reference to any specific connection between the death of Jesus and the forgiveness of sins or justification, but it gave Paul the assurance that Jesus was God's supreme revealer and agent, who, by giving Himself in life and death, had given men a truth of God that triumphed in their hearts. And this is only to put into other words the gospel that Jesus saves us because, by all that He

resurrection of the dead." This aspect of the resurrection has been dealt with elsewhere (p. 60) : we saw that it was closely connected with the fact and nature of Jesus' death. In any case the importance of the resurrection to Paul and his fellow-apostles was in the character of the Man whose resurrection they proclaimed and especially in the manner of His death.

It is hardly necessary to say that Paul connects the salvation that Jesus brings to men with His death. To Paul, Jesus is the One " who gave Himself up for me " (Gal. ii. 20) : a fellow-man is one " for whose sake Christ died " (1 Cor. viii. 11). He connects man's salvation especially with Jesus' dying " for sins,"—" The gospel which I preached unto you . . . how that Christ died for our sins according to the scriptures " (1 Cor. xv. 1, 3).

But when we ask how Paul thought of Jesus as dying for our sins we note first he looks upon Jesus' death as one with His life. He gives no hint of thinking that Jesus' relationship to sin and to God was other in His death than in His life. And the emphasis is always upon the Man who died rather than upon His death,—" We preach Christ crucified " (1 Cor. i. 23) : " I determined not to know anything among you save Jesus Christ, and Him crucified " (1 Cor. ii. 2) : " God, sending His own Son in the likeness of sinful flesh, and for sin, condemned sin in the flesh " (Rom. viii. 3). It is the Man rather than His death that saves and mediates,—" Christ Jesus came into the world to save sinners " (1 Tim. i. 15) : " one mediator also between God and man, Himself man, Christ Jesus, who gave Himself a ransom for all " (1 Tim. ii. 5). His death was the culmination of His life's obedience,—" Through the obedience of the one shall the many be made righteous " (Rom. v. 19) : " Taking the form of a servant . . . becoming obedient unto death, yea, the death of the cross " (Phil. ii. 7, 8). And in His death God was with Him as in His life,—" God was in Christ reconciling the world unto Himself " (2 Cor. v. 19) ; nor does Paul suggest anything else even when he speaks of Jesus' death as sacrifice,—" Christ also loved you, and gave Himself up for us, an offering and a sacrifice to God for an odour of a sweet smell " (Eph. v. 2).

Paul speaks of Jesus' relationship to sin in His death as being what ours ought to be,—" The death that He died, He died unto sin once . . . even so reckon ye also yourselves to be dead unto sin " (Rom. vi. 10, 11). He reckons his own sufferings for the Church as " filling up on his part that which is lacking of the afflictions of Christ " (Col. i. 24).

When we ask what Paul thought of the relationship of the death of Jesus to the salvation of man we must first (having already dealt with his use of the term " justification ") consider what he meant by " recon- ciliation," for his meaning of the word seems to vary. In Rom. v. 10 he writes, " For if, while we were enemies we were reconciled to God through the death of His Son, much more, being reconciled, shall we be saved by His life." Here " reconciliation " is much the same as the " justification " of the prior verse, distinct from salvation and little more than a formal preliminary to it (cf. Rom. xi. 15, where " the casting away of Israel " is " the reconciliation of the world "). But this formal distinction of reconciliation from salvation and the attaching of the former to the death and the latter to the life of Jesus seems to be for the purposes of the dialectic upon justification, on which Paul was engaged in the Roman letter. Paul's more intimate thinking appears when, envisag- ing the whole range of God's renewing help for man, he writes (2 Cor. v. 19) : " God was in Christ recon-

that the life also of Jesus may be manifested in our body " (2 Cor. iv. 10), and of " the fellowship of His sufferings, becoming conformed unto His death " (Phil. iii. 10).

If we needed any further proof that Paul's most vital thought of the death of Jesus was expressed in terms of fellowship rather than substitution, we should find it in noting that it was the fellowship of the believer with his Lord in death that lay behind Paul's characteristic phrase of being " in Christ " or of Christ being " in " the believer. " I have been crucified with Christ, yet I live, and yet no longer I, Christ liveth in me " (Gal. ii. 20). It is by help of this thought that he turns in the Epistle to the Romans from the forensic to the vital,—" There is therefore now no condemnation to them that are in Christ Jesus " (Rom. viii. 1).

And of what he means by this fellowship of the believer with Jesus in death and life Paul gives us more than a hint. When he writes that " the *word* of the cross is to them that are perishing foolishness, but unto us which are being saved it is the power of God " (1 Cor. i. 18), he declares that the cross saves as a revealer of the truth about God, which truth becomes the power of God, so that " Christ crucified " is " Christ the power of God, and the wisdom of God " (1 Cor. i. 24). But Jesus is more than a transparency through which men see God : His death gives Him a lordship over the human heart : " To this end Christ died, and lived again, that He might be Lord of both the dead and the living " (Rom. xiv. 9). The power of His lordship is given in a more intimate way in 2 Cor. v. 14, " The love of Christ constraineth us ; because we thus judge, that One died for all, therefore all died ; and He died for all, that they which live should no longer live unto themselves, but unto Him who for their sakes died and rose again." And in Jesus' crowning act of self-giving, which overcomes the selfishness of the human heart, God is known and triumphs over the sin that withheld man from his true allegiance,—" God commendeth His own love toward us, in that, while we were yet sinners, Christ died for us " (Rom. v. 8).

And it will be seen that in these phrases, where the heart and experience of Paul speak most feelingly and simply, we have little more than a reiteration of the gospel that Jesus preached. The chief difference lies in the emphasis put upon the death of Jesus, which becomes the strongest expression and surest proof and most intimate embodiment of the truth of God which was His gospel. Jesus proclaimed a God who sought the lost and who loved the evil and unthankful ; the significance of Jesus' death to Paul was that it made him sure that God did so love the sinner. Jesus, by all that He did and was and suffered, achieved so complete a kingship in the hearts of His followers that His truth of God did actually reign in them and to that extent established the kingdom of God on earth. Paul found his conversion by accepting the kingship of Jesus, which brought an effective enthronement of God in his heart and made his life an ambassage.

(5) THE ACTS OF THE APOSTLES.

In considering the gospel as it appears in the book of Acts, we are reminded that modern means for verbatim reporting did not exist when that book was written, and that ancient historians commonly themselves composed the speeches which they put into the mouths of historic persons. To what extent this is true of Acts cannot be discussed here. But even if it is far more extensively true than seems probable, we have at least what the historian thought his characters thought or what he himself thought. In so far, therefore, as the book is not evidence for the thought of the Apostles, it is evidence for the thought of the generation to which they ministered, and this for our general purpose would be almost as valuable.

The following features mark the gospel as it appears in the Acts :—

(a) The specific message of the Apostles is the Messiahship of Jesus. "Let all the house of Israel know assuredly, that God hath made Him both Lord and Christ, this Jesus whom ye crucified " (ii. 36) : "They ceased not to teach and to preach Jesus as the Christ " (v. 42 : see also viii. 5, 37 ; xvii, 3, 7 ; xviii. 5, 28).

(b) The death of Jesus is not brought into special connection with the remission of sins, but is regularly used to convict and discredit the existing Jewish religious authorities, the resurrection being appealed to as God's reversal of the Jewish condemnation of Jesus (Acts ii. 23, 24 ; iii. 13, 14, 15, 17 ; iv. 10 ; v. 28, 30, 31 ; vii. 52 ; x. 39, 40 ; xiii. 27, 30). When Isa. liii. is interpreted as prophetic of the death of Jesus (Acts viii. 30–38), there is no hint that it was understood in the sense of the traditional gospel, nor are those parts of this chapter mentioned on which the traditional gospel lays special stress. Neither when Paul speaks to the elders of Miletus of " the Church of the Lord which He purchased with His own blood " (xx. 28) nor when, before Agrippa, in describing his gospel, he declares "how that the Christ must suffer " (xxvi. 23) is the death of Jesus connected with the forgiveness of sins.

(c) Remission of sins is connected, not with the death of Jesus, but with baptism in His name (ii. 38,

xxii. 16), or with repentance (iii. 19, v. 31, viii. 22)
xi. 18, xxvi. 18), or with belief in Jesus stated generally
without special reference to His death (x. 43, xiii. 38).

(d) The gospel which the Apostles preached was
assumed to be one with the gospel that Jesus
preached. Peter (x. 36 ff.) speaks definitely of the
gospel as being that which Jesus proclaimed. The
apostolic gospel is the gospel of the kingdom (viii. 12,
xix. 8, xxviii, 23, 31; also i. 3, 6). What salvation
through belief in Jesus meant appears in the story
of the Philippian jailor : he is told, " Believe on the
Lord Jesus, and thou shalt be saved, thou and thy
house " (xvi. 31), and his response is recorded in the
statement that they " believed in God " (v. 34 ; see
also xxvi. 23).

It is very clear, therefore, that the gospel which the
author of Acts believed to have been preached by
the apostles was very much nearer to the gospel that
Jesus preached than to the traditional gospel. Its
central proclamation was that Jesus was Christ and
Lord : and though a good deal is said about the
remission of sins, there is no hint that the death of
Jesus was held to be a necessary condition for
forgiveness.

And if we bear in mind that Paul found (Gal. ii.
1, 2) his gospel to be in substantial agreement with
the gospel of the other apostles and that the author
of Acts, if not a companion of Paul, was at least
under Pauline influence, we shall find in this examination of Acts a confirmation of the conclusion reached
in the consideration of Paul's gospel.

(6) THE FIRST THREE GOSPELS.

For our purpose the evidence of the first three
Gospels has more than one aspect. In so far as we

accept them as authentic records of the words and acts of Jesus, they bear upon what has already been said (in Chapter II) about Jesus' gospel and His own understanding of His death. But these documents must also be considered as evidence of their writers' conception of the gospel of Jesus. The selection of what is recorded reflects the mind of the evangelist or of those from whom he had his tradition. A still clearer reflection of this is found when there is reason to think that the form or substance of a saying or narrative has been modified. Sometimes also we have the evangelist's own comments. And in considering the Second and Third Gospels we have to take into account the alleged Pauline influence, which, so far as it exists, makes them subsidiary evidence for his thought.

Much of what is common to the first three Gospels has been treated in Chapter II, so that we need here note only those points that indicate their individual attitude.

(a) Mark.

In the Second Gospel, which is generally considered our best authority for the facts of Jesus' life, He appears pre-eminently as the preacher of the gospel and as the Christ.

Jesus' own words tell us that it was for the task of preaching the gospel that He left privacy,—" Let us go elsewhere into the next towns, that I may preach there also ; for to this end came I forth " (i. 38) ; and the circumstances of this saying, together with other sayings and acts (i. 40–45, iii. 9, with which cf. iv. 1, viii. 22–26), tell us that, despite the prominence given in the Gospel to miracles, Jesus found that His popularity as a healer hindered His proper work of preaching. And in the evangelist's words, as in Jesus' own words, it is as preacher that He came from privacy : " Now after that John was delivered up, Jesus came into Galilee, preaching the gospel of God " (i. 14).

The Messiahship of Jesus is the central assertion of the Second Evangelist and the central element in his idea of the gospel. This is evident in the title, if it is his, " The beginning of the gospel of Jesus Christ, the Son of God " (" Son of God " being probably used here in the sense of xiv. 61 as a synonym of " the Christ "). The beginning of Jesus' vocation as preacher of the gospel of God (i. 14, 15) is in the Messianic experience of the voice at baptism, " Thou art My beloved Son, in Thee I am well pleased " (i. 11). The critical point of His ministry is Peter's confession, " Thou art the Christ " (viii. 29). And He lays down His life by confessing " I am " to the high priest's question, " Art Thou the Christ, the Son of the Blessed ? " (xiv. 61).

There is much in the book about the forgiveness of sins but no hint of the death of Jesus as a necessary condition thereto. John " preached the baptism of repentance unto remission of sins " (i. 4). Jesus said to the paralytic, " Thy sins are forgiven " (ii. 5), and when challenged as to the validity of His words He appeals not to any sacrificial death but to His present power in the man (ii. 9). The possibility of forgiveness is discussed without any reference to what the traditional gospel claims to be its only and necessary condition (iii. 28–30). The way of forgiveness is defined : " Whensoever ye stand praying, forgive, if ye have aught against any one ; that your Father also which is in heaven may forgive you your trespasses " (xi. 25). Jesus tells the ruler how he may " inherit eternal life," and there is no mention of any such condition as the traditional gospel demands.

(b) " Q."

Before considering the First and Third Gospels by themselves we need to look at those sections which they have in common with each other but not with Mark. It is generally now concluded that these passages came from a common source (designated by the symbol " Q "), which therefore ranks with or even above Mark in primitiveness and authenticity.

Of course, we do not know how much there may have been in " Q " for which neither Matthew nor Luke found room, but even when all allowance under this head is made it is remarkable that in " Q " the only saying of Jesus that refers to His death is, " Whosoever doth not take up his cross and follow Me is not worthy of Me " (Matt. x. 38, Luke xiv. 27). The saying suggests that Jesus regarded Himself, no less in death than in life, rather as the leader than as the substitute of His followers. This accords exactly with the Marcan account that Jesus commonly spoke of Himself, especially in predicting His suffering, under the Danielic figure of " Son of man," which symbolized the " saints of the Most High " (see pp. 31 ff.).

As in Mark, so here, the possibilities of forgiveness are set forth without any reference to sacrifice or propitiation by Himself (Matt. xii. 32, Luke xii. 10). Our willingness to forgive is made the one condition of our being forgiven (Matt. vi. 12, Luke xi. 4), and this principle is given in the more general form, " Judge not, and ye shall not be judged " (Matt. vii. 1, Luke vi. 37). It should be noted that this last saying brings the teaching of Jesus to a point where we cannot avoid direct comparison and contrast with the Pauline doctrine of justification by faith.

As in Mark, Jesus is especially the preacher of the

gospel. The culminating evidence of His Messiahship to the messengers of the Baptist is that " the
poor have the gospel preached unto them " (Matt. xi. 5,
Luke vii. 22), and the gospel, we learn from the
message with which the Twelve were sent, was the
gospel of the nearness of the kingdom of God
(Matt. x. 7, Luke ix. 2).

Many of the most significant citations made in
Chapter II are drawn from " Q " :—

The least in the kingdom is greater than John
(Matt. xi. 11, Luke vii. 28) :

Jesus' power to help man against evil is the evidence
of the kingdom's nearness (Matt. xii. 28, Luke xi. 20) :
the Twelve are privileged to see that for which the
ages have waited (Matt. xiii. 16, 17, Luke x. 23, 24) :
Jesus is conscious of unique knowledge of God (Matt.
xi. 27, Luke x. 22) :

God loves the evil and unjust as well as the just
and good (Matt. v. 45, Luke vi. 35) ; and, like the
shepherd, God's greatest concern is for those who are
farthest from Him (Matt. xviii. 10–14, Luke xv. 3–7,
the last verse of both of these passages making it
clear that the shepherd stands for God) ;

And man's salvation lies in the hearing and doing
of the word of Jesus (Matt. vii. 24–27, Luke vi. 46–49).

(c) Matthew.

We have now to deal only with what is peculiar to
Matthew and Luke, having already dealt with what
is common to both of them (" Q ") and also with what
they share with Mark. And in this respect there is
little in the First Gospel that needs consideration.

We note the phrase " the gospel of the kingdom "
(iv. 23, ix. 35, xxiv. 14).

We have already seen (pp. 44 f.) that to the Marcan
account of the Lord's supper the First Gospel adds

the words, " unto remission of sins," while from the Marcan account of the Baptist's preaching it omits these same words, which indicates an attitude of mind not shared by the other evangelists. This, however, may be the work of a later editor rather than that of the evangelist to whom we owe the general compilation of the book. For even what is peculiar to it contains much that is incompatible with the idea that a sacrifice of any sort is necessary for the forgiveness of sins :—

(*a*) " Go ye and learn what this meaneth, I desire mercy and not sacrifice ; for I came not to call the righteous, but sinners " (ix. 13) :

(*b*) With peculiar emphasis it is stated that the condition of being forgiven is to forgive (vi. 14, 15 ; xviii. 35). The same principle is applied, from the offender's point of view, to the Temple offerings (v. 23, 24), is included in the beatitude, " Blessed are the merciful, for they shall obtain mercy " (v. 7), and in xviii. 22–34 is embodied in a parable.

(*c*) In xxv. 31–46 we have a picture of the judgment in which the fate of man is shown to depend upon whether he has been merciful or not. The genuineness of this passage has been challenged, and it has been contended that we have here, as in certain portions of Mark xiii., a fragment of Jewish apocalyptic inserted amongst the sayings of Jesus. But if this is so, it tells us what the evangelist who was responsible for its insertion thought to be genuine Christian teaching and makes it quite clear that his idea of the means of salvation was not that of the traditional gospel.

(*d*) At the end of the Gospel we read, " And Jesus came unto them and spake unto them, saying, All authority hath been given unto Me in heaven and on earth (cf. Matt. xi. 27, Luke x. 22). Go ye therefore, and make disciples of all nations, baptizing them into the name of the Father and of the Son and of the Holy Spirit : teaching them to observe all things whatsoever I commanded you : and lo, I am with you alway, even unto the end of the world " (cf. Matt. x. 40, Luke x. 16). With the exception of the baptism clause, these words might stand as a summary of the teaching of Jesus as recorded in " Q," and they represent the evangelist's conviction as to the mission and message of the Church. It is interesting to note how close the contents of this commission are to those of Paul's Damascene experience : we have the lordship of Jesus (Acts ix. 5), the oneness of Jesus with His followers (ibid.), and the universal commission (Acts ix. 15, xxvi. 16–18). And since the First Gospel probably represents a Palestinian tradition, we have here a corroboration of Paul's statement that the gospel which was revealed to him from heaven was found by him to be the same as that which the apostles at Jerusalem were preaching (Gal. i. 11, 12 ; ii. 2). It is obvious that no one who held the traditional view of the gospel could have given such a summary of the Church's mission and message as these verses (Matt. xxviii. 18–20), where there is no mention at all of what the adherents of the traditional gospel claim to be essential to man's salvation and central in Jesus' work.

(d) Luke.

As Matthew, so Luke, in what is peculiar to his gospel, does not add much that bears upon our subject, but what is added confirms our general conclusions.

In iv. 17–21 we have Jesus' declaration of His vocation as a preacher,—" And He opened the book, and found the place where it was written, The Spirit of the Lord is upon Me, because He hath anointed Me to preach good tidings to the poor. . . . And He began to say unto them, To-day hath this scripture been fulfilled in your ears."

The preaching of both Jesus and His disciples is described as " the gospel of the kingdom of God " (iv. 43, viii. 1, ix. 2, x. 9, 11).

We may note two passages that approximate to the Johannine idea of Jesus' death as being His glorifying,—" When the days were well-nigh come that He should be received up " (ix. 51) and " Behoved it not the Christ to suffer these things and to enter into His glory ? " (xxiv. 26), an idea that represents Jesus' doctrine of kingship through service and suffering.

Zacharias' prophecy (i. 77) confirms, as against Matthew's account, the place of the remission of sins in John's preaching.

The story of the woman that was a sinner (vii. 36–50) and Jesus' prayer upon the cross (xxiii. 34) are two very intimate utterances upon forgiveness, neither of which suggests that Jesus held to the conditions for which the traditional gospel stipulates. To the sayings recorded in Matthew a still further generalization of the conditions of forgiveness is added, " Condemn not, and ye shall not be condemned : release and ye shall be released " (vi. 37). And we must note that though verse 38 may be read to suggest that the reciprocity promised is human, we see in vi. 22, 23, 34, that a human return is not to be looked for and that therefore vi. 37, 38 must be understood to speak ultimately of the relationship between man and God.

It is penitence that justifies (xviii. 14). It is the repentance of the sinner that gladdens God (xv. 7,

10) and that calls forth Jesus' words to Zacchæus,
" To-day is salvation come to this house " (xix. 9).
In the closing charge to the disciples repentance alone
is mentioned as the preliminary to remission, and, as
such, repentance is to be preached in the name of
Jesus,—" that repentance and " or " unto " " remission of sins should be preached in His name unto all
nations " (xxiv. 47). The meaning seems to be that
all that Jesus was in life and death and all that He
made known of God should be powerful to move men
to an entire change of mind which should bring a
life-giving fellowship with God. Repentance is thus,
as elsewhere in this Gospel, the simple human response
to divine love. It is the memory of his father that
turns the prodigal home again. In the parable of
the lost coin as in that of the lost sheep it is rather
God that seeks man till He finds than man that turns
to God. And the story of Zacchæus ends with the
saying, " For the Son of man is come to seek and to
save that which was lost " (xix. 10).

Thus Luke also shows that the gospel of the
primitive Church was substantially the gospel that
Jesus preached and was a very different thing from
the traditional gospel of the later Church.

(7) The First Epistle of Peter.

The First Epistle of Peter is particularly illuminating as to early Christian thought upon the death
of Jesus.

We may probably take the reference to the death of
Jesus in the epistolary greeting as giving the aspect
of it that was dominant in the writer's mind. Here
we have the repetition of Jesus' own thought ; for
" unto obedience and sprinkling of the blood of Jesus
Christ " (i. 2) refers obviously to the covenant-making
obedience and sprinkling of Exod. xxiv. 7, 8, and

so takes up in other language the figure of " This cup is the new covenant in My blood."

In i. 18, 19 we have another figure, " Ye were redeemed . . . from your vain manner of life handed down from your fathers . . . with precious blood, as of a lamb without blemish and without spot, even the blood of Christ." The meaning is made quite clear,— the death of Jesus is a costly but effective means of bringing man into touch with reality. The positive side of this boon is that " through Him ye are believers in God " (v. 21). And the passage closes by describing the gospel as the living and eternal life-giving word of God (i. 23–25). It is by obedience to this truth that they purified their souls (i. 22), and later (iv. 17) we read of the gospel as demanding, not faith only, but obedience.

Of especial interest are two passages that let us know what was meant by saying that Jesus suffered for sins :—

We read : " For it is better, if the will of God so will, that ye suffer for well-doing than for evil-doing. Because Christ also suffered for sins once, the just for the unjust, that He might bring us to God " (iii. 17, 18), where the writer implies that Jesus' " suffering for sins " was analogous to the Christian's experience of suffering wrongfully. The same connection of thought is found in ii. 20, " If, when ye do well and suffer for it, ye take it patiently, this is acceptable with God. For hereunto were ye called ; because Christ also suffered for you." The writer goes on to tell us that Jesus, " when He suffered threatened not ; but committed Himself to Him that judgeth righteously," and thus he makes it clear that he regarded Jesus' sufferings as having been inflicted by men, and did not understand Jesus in His suffering to have felt Himself condemned by

God. And it is significant also that in ii. 24 where he uses the words, " by whose stripes ye were healed," which by themselves might be construed into a statement of substitutionary suffering, he places them in a context which excludes such import ; for they are an appendix to the fuller statement that Jesus " His own self bare our sins in His body upon the tree, that we, having died unto sins, might live unto righteousness," which gives us the idea of fellowship rather than substitution.

(8) THE EPISTLE TO THE HEBREWS.

In no New Testament writing is the interpretation of the death of Jesus as a sacrifice for sins so fully elaborated as in the Epistle to the Hebrews. But it is very interesting to mark that this elaboration is found in the latter part of the tract, when the writer has " ceased to speak of the first principles of Christ " (vi. 1). So that we must expect on the whole to find his gospel before this point. And the first five chapters have two dominant thoughts :—

(1) The " great salvation " that comes through Jesus is that " which having at the first been spoken through the Lord, was confirmed unto us by them that heard " (ii. 3) ; that is, it was what Jesus preached. This is but another aspect of the declaration with which his treatise opens, " God . . . hath at the end of these days spoken unto us in a Son " (i. 1, 2).

(2) In ii. 9, 10 the author states what the death of Jesus means to him : " We behold . . . Jesus, because of the suffering of death crowned with glory and honour, that by the grace of God He should taste death for every man. For it became Him, for whom are all things, and through whom are all things, in bringing many sons unto glory, to make the author," or rather " prince " or " leader," " of their salvation

perfect through sufferings." " Perfect " in this connection evidently means perfect in the captaincy or leadership of man's salvation. Jesus' sufferings and death are the means to an effective kingship and leadership of mankind in the things of God. Such a statement is an echo of Jesus' own thought, and expresses the simple experience of the human heart in the contemplation of His death. The writer continues in the same strain, " that through death He might bring to nought him that hath the power of death, that is, the devil ; and might deliver all them who through fear of death were all their lifetime subject to bondage " (ii. 14, 15), which repeats the thought of Jesus, " The Son of man came . . . to give His life a ransom for many."

Where in this section (Chapters I–V) he mentions " propitiation " (ii. 17) it is by a curious anticipation of one of the chief figures of his later elaboration, the high priest. The point of connection is that, having spoken of the mercy and faithfulness of Jesus, he turns aside to say that it is necessary for a high priest to be " merciful and faithful," " for in that He Himself hath suffered being tempted, He is able to succour them that are tempted." But such a qualification and duty have nothing to do with the Mosaic priesthood. The violence and artificiality of this transition from the ethical and spiritual to the ritual suggests that the real substratum of the writer's thought rests on the former and has no vital connection with the ritual figures of propitiation and priesthood.

The fundamental thought of ii. 9, 10 as to the death of Jesus is repeated in v. 8, 9, " Though He was a Son, yet learned obedience by the things which He suffered ; and having been made perfect, He became unto all them that obey Him the author " or causative personality " of eternal salvation." In both passages Jesus' sufferings are regarded as in line with the obedience and task of His life. They give Him a saving ascendancy over man's heart.

We have here a presentation of the saving power of Jesus Christ which is very much nearer to the gospel that He preached than to the traditional gospel. And our understanding of the writer's meaning is confirmed by his specification of " the first principles of Christ " in vi. 1, 2,—" of repentance from dead works, and of faith toward God, of the teaching of baptisms, and of laying on of hands, and of resurrection of the dead, and of eternal judgment." Such a statement of " first principles " or " elementary doctrine " " of Christ " must comprise the writer's gospel and, since the ritual and eschatological items could not come under this term, we must find it in the power of Jesus to move men to " repentance and faith toward God."

In the closing and more hortative chapters of his work, where the author is concerned to speak of the death of Jesus apart from the development of any special piece of symbolism, his thought reverts repeatedly to Jesus' own figure of the blood-covenant,— " The blood of the covenant wherewith He was sanctified " (x. 29), " to Jesus the mediator of a new covenant and to the blood of sprinkling that speaketh better than that of Abel " (xii. 24), " Who brought again from the dead the great Shepherd of the sheep with the blood of the eternal covenant " (xiii. 20).

The writer hints that the second part of his tract (chap. vi ff.) is to consist of " solid food for full-grown men who by reason of use have their senses exercised to discern good and evil " (v. 14). This is a warning that he intends to use methods of thought and speech that are not simple and perspicuous. He proceeds to elaborate an apologetic which amounts to an attempt to prove the validity of the Christian faith from the data of the commonly accepted Jewish tenets as to the divine origin of the Mosaic ritual and as to the verbal inspiration of the scriptures, and he employs for this purpose the contemporary fashion of allegorical interpretation.

Perhaps we should rather say that he proceeds to illustrate the office and death of Jesus by symbolic and allegorical use of the Old Testament and especially of its ritual material in a way that shows the need of the caution suggested on pp. 61 f. For it is hardly courteous to take as intended for serious reasoning the writer's contention that because the death of Melchizedek is not recorded, he therefore did not die, and that because his parents are never mentioned that therefore he had none (vii. 3, 8) ; or that Levi paid tithes to Melchizedek because Abraham paid them before Levi was born ; or that, since the Greek word for " testament " and " covenant " are the same, therefore, because a will or testament does not come into force till after the death of the testator, it follows that a covenant cannot be " dedicated without blood " (ix. 15–18). Of course, serious reasoning may lie behind such a play of figures, but we shall wrong the writer if we depend on them for the clue to his thought.

These cautions must therefore be borne in mind when we turn to consider the arguments concerning the death of Jesus which are found in Chapters IX and X, where the author undertakes to relate the Christian faith to the Jewish sacrificial system by regarding the latter as the shadow of the former. He begins by reminding his readers that " according to the law, I may almost say, all things are cleansed with blood, and apart from shedding of blood there is no remission " (ix. 22). From what is necessary in the shadow it is argued that " the heavenly things themselves " must be cleansed " with better sacrifices than these " (v. 23)—though he does not say how " the heavenly things " came to need cleansing,—and therefore " now once at the end of the ages " Christ " hath been manifested to put away sin by the sacrifice of Himself " (v. 26). But now, having argued the necessity of the sacrifice of Jesus from the Mosaic principle that " without shedding of blood there is no remission," he goes on to state the futility of the Mosaic method,—" It is impossible that the blood of bulls and goats should take away sins " (x. 4), and proves from the Psalms that what God required was not sacrifice but the will to do His will (v. 5–9), which demand was fulfilled in Jesus ; and immediately he describes the content of Jesus' will as being to offer Himself as a sacrifice for sins (v. 10, 12). The writer seems to be trying at one and the same time to prove the inadequacy and unspirituality of the Mosaic ritual of remission and to use its principles and methods as data for Christian apologetic. He confesses the moral and spiritual futility of the Mosaic sacrifice (x. 4) and yet applies its terms and ideas to that which supersedes it (x. 10–12).

Two other instances of this strange mingling of incompatible modes of thought may be noted. In ix. 13–14 the skeleton of the argument is, " If the blood of goats and bulls . . . sanctify unto the cleanness of the flesh : how much more shall the blood of Christ . . . cleanse your conscience . . . ? " The Mosaic notion that the blood of a victim brought into physical contact with the person had power to make his body ritually clean is accepted as an agreed basis, and from this it is argued that the blood of Christ

with no such physical contact could produce moral
cleansing in that which is spirit and not body. This
is evidently not argument but poetic analogy, which
becomes the more evident when we restore the
attendant clauses. For " cleansing from dead works
to serve the living God " is rather quickening than
cleansing, and spiritual quickening is the work, not
of blood but of spirit, as the writer is careful to suggest when he goes on to speak of " the blood of
Christ who through the eternal Spirit offered Himself
without blemish unto God." By this strange mingling
of the figurative and direct use of language the ethical
and spiritual idea of self-devotion is brought into
verbal connection with the ritual formalities of animal
sacrifice.

So also in xiii. 10–12 the author of this tract states
the incompatibility of the Mosaic animal sacrifice
with the following of Jesus, and then appeals to an
element of that ritual as giving the reason for the
place of Jesus' death,—" The bodies of those beasts,
whose blood is brought into the holy place by the
high priest as an offering for sin, are burned without
the camp. Wherefore Jesus also, that He might
sanctify the people through His own blood, suffered
without the gate." But how much of this is poetry
and how little it is intended for strict reasoning is
revealed by the sequel, " Let us therefore go forth
unto Him without the camp, bearing His reproach "
(v. 13).

We see, then, that to the writer of this treatise the
gospel of the Church was that which came from the
lips of Jesus. Its power lies in bringing men to
repentance and faith toward God. When he speaks
simply and directly of the death of Jesus, he regards
it as the culmination of His obedience to God and
as that which made Him the effective leader of men

in the things of God. And where he speaks of it in the terms of sacrifice, his strange use of figurative language compels us to understand his figures in the light of his more directly and simply expressed thought.

(9) THE APOCALYPSE.

The writer to the Hebrews regarded the Mosaic ritual as the shadow of the things in heaven : the Apocalyptist sees the heavenlies themselves under Mosaic forms. But though the Apocalypse is said to be the most Jewish book in the New Testament, its allusions to the death of Jesus seem to exclude the interpretation of it as a sin-offering.

An expression such as " who loveth us and loosed us from our sins by His blood " (i. 5) implies rather actual liberation from sin than acquittal from guilt. When we read, " These are they that came out of great tribulation, and they washed their robes, and made them white in the blood of the Lamb " (vii. 14), it seems that we must understand the white robe to symbolize victory rather than pardon (cf. v. 9, " arrayed in white robes and palms in their hands ") and to be a figurative rendering of Paul's " more than conquerors through Him that loved us." This thought recurs in xii. 11, " And they overcame him because of the blood of the Lamb."

In v. 9, 10 we read, " Thou wast slain, and didst purchase unto God with Thy blood men of every tribe, and tongue, and people, and nation, and madest them to be unto our God a kingdom and priests." It is clear that in speaking here of blood and of the Lamb slain the Apocalyptist is not thinking of Jesus' death as a sin-offering, but rather as something done for God at great cost that wins men from all that withholds them from God and so brings them into

His kingdom. We have the same thought in his vision, " I saw in the midst of the throne . . . a Lamb standing as though it had been slain " (v. 6), for it is in the death of Jesus that God is enthroned in men's hearts. It is possible that he draws the form of his figure from the covenant sacrifice.

But " the Lamb . . . hath been slain from the foundation of the world " (xiii. 8) ; the inference from which is that in the mind of the Apocalyptist Jesus' death is the revelation of the eternal truth of God and is so because of His utter loyalty to God in face of all that denied His truth. And we find con firmation of this in the unusual phrase, " Jesus Christ, the faithful witness, the firstborn of the dead " (i. 5, cf. iii. 14, " These things saith the faithful and true witness "). For in this writer the word translated " witness " ($\mu\acute{\alpha}\rho\tau\upsilon\varsigma$) elsewhere means " martyr " (ii. 13, xi. 3, xvii. 6), and also the reference to the resurrection (" the firstborn of the dead ") suggests that " faithful witness " means " faithful unto death." And a similar understanding of Jesus' death, linking the idea of " the faithful witness " to that of " the Lamb in the midst of the throne " is found in iii. 21, " He that overcometh, I will give to him to sit down with Me in My throne, as I also overcame, and sat down with My Father in His throne."

Thus we find that in the Apocalypse the dominant thought of the death of Jesus is that of power and victory, the power and victory of God's eternally self-giving love made known and effective in the death to which Jesus was brought by His utter loyalty to the truth of God.

(10) THE FOURTH GOSPEL.

An appeal to the Fourth Gospel as evidence for the exact words and deeds of Jesus is not likely to be unchallenged. To-day even those who accept it as the work of the son of Zebedee are generally willing to allow that to some extent it represents rather his experience of the present and glorified Christ than his memory of Jesus. But apart from its value as history, its place in Christian devotion as " the spiritual gospel " and its value as evidence of early Christian thought make it extremely interesting and important for our present purpose.

The gospel is almost as remarkable for its omissions as for its contents. Only once is forgiveness of sins spoken of,—" Whose soever sins ye forgive, they are forgiven unto them ; whose soever sins ye retain, they are retained " (xx. 23), a saying which, whatever it means, is hardly compatible with the idea of forgiveness contained in the traditional gospel.

In view of the omission of all direct reference to the Lord's supper, the language of vi. 32–58 has often been interpreted as bearing upon it. Whether this is correct or not, it should be noted that the eating of the flesh and the drinking of the blood of the Son of man is here connected, not with the covenant sacrifice and still less with the sin-offering, but with the miraculous feeding of the multitude and with the Israelites' eating of manna in the wilderness. The death of Jesus is presented here, not in the terms of sacrifice but under the figure of food and drink in their life-giving power. And in verse 63 we are told that Jesus, in speaking of His flesh, was speaking of the truth by which He lived,—" The flesh profiteth nothing : the words that I speak unto you are spirit and are life." He thus ends with a more explicit declaration of the idea from which the discourse began, " He that cometh unto Me shall not hunger, and he that believeth on Me shall never thirst " (vi. 35 ; see p. 43).

In two passages only is the idea of animal sacrifice connected with the death of Jesus. In i. 29 the Baptist says, " Behold, the Lamb of God, which taketh away the sin of the world," but in v. 33–36 Jesus' appeal to the Baptist's witness is described as a concession to Jewish ideas,—" The witness which I receive is not from man : howbeit I say these things, that ye may be saved." This attitude accords precisely with what we have been led to conclude should be the way to regard the earliest application of the term " sin-offering " to the death of Jesus, i.e. as an association of thought, helpful and natural to Jews, but not intrinsically illuminative. In xix. 36 we read, " For these things came to pass, that the scripture might be fulfilled, A bone of Him shall not be broken." The allusion is to the paschal lamb ; but the paschal lamb was not a sin-offering and approximated rather to the covenant sacrifice. Its chief significance was apparently that those who participated belonged to the people of Jehovah,— " This is the ordinance of the passover : there shall no alien eat thereof. . . . All the congregation of Israel shall keep it " (Exod. xii. 43, 47). " The blood shall be to you for a token upon the houses where ye are " (Exod. xii. 13).

Elsewhere, in the discourses of the Fourth Gospel, there are many references by Jesus to His death, but all of them bring it into specific relation with other things than the remission of sins :—

(a) In three places the " lifting up " of the Son of man or of Jesus is spoken of. The evangelist, in xii. 33, explains this as a prophecy of the elevation of the body on the cross, but the meaning seems to be wider and to include the spiritual exaltation after and through His death. In no case is it connected with forgiveness. In iii. 14, 15 it is the occasion of

belief and the means of life,—"As Moses lifted up
the serpent in the wilderness, even so must the Son
of man be lifted up : that whosoever believeth may
in Him have eternal life." In viii. 28 it is the evidence of Jesus' Messiahship, i.e. of His complete
subservience to God,—"When ye have lifted up the
Son of man, then shall ye know that I am He, and that
I do nothing of Myself" (cf. xiv. 31). In xii. 32
Jesus speaks of His "lifting up" as a means to
power. "I, if I be lifted up from the earth, will
draw all men unto Myself." And we have an echo
of this aspect of Jesus' death in the evangelist's own
words, that Jesus died "that He might also gather
together into one the children of God that are
scattered abroad" (xi. 52).

(b) "The good shepherd layeth down His life for
the sheep" (x. 11). Jesus' death proves His complete devotion as contrasted with the hireling "whose
own the sheep are not," and so establishes the right-
fulness of His authority (cf. viii. 28 as above).

(c) "Except a grain of wheat fall into the earth
and die, it abideth by itself alone ; but if it die, it
beareth much fruit" (xii. 24). The life-giving power
of Jesus' death is here spoken of in close connection
with the principle which He gave His followers,
"He that loveth his life loseth it . . ." (xii. 25,
Mark viii. 35, etc.), and with the lifting up of the Son
of man (John xii. 32).

(d) In closest connection with the foregoing, the
death of Jesus is also spoken of as the glorifying of the
Son of man and of God in Him (xii. 23, 27, 28, and
also xiii. 31).

(e) In xiv. 31 He says, as He goes to His arrest,
"That the world may know that I love the Father,
and as the Father hath given Me commandment, even
so I do."

(*f*) Again, in xv. 13 His death is evidence of His love to His followers, " Greater love hath no man than this, that a man lay down his life for his friends."

(*g*) His death is necessary for making His truth truly inward to His followers,—" If I go not away, the Comforter will not come unto you " (xvi. 7), which may be compared with " Except ye eat the flesh of the Son of man and drink His blood, ye have not life in yourselves " (vi. 53).

With regard to salvation from sin, we read that the soul is cleansed by the truth taught by Jesus,— " Already ye are clean because of the word which I have spoken unto you " (xv. 3). So, too, we read, " Sanctify them in the truth " (xvii. 17), " The truth shall make you free " (viii. 32). The belief that saves is the belief that Jesus was sent of God, i.e. was the Christ,—" Except ye believe that I am He, ye shall die in your sins " (viii. 24) : " The Father Himself loveth you, because ye have loved Me, and have believed that I came forth from the Father " (xvi. 27) : " They believed that Thou didst send Me " (xvii. 8).

The fundamental affirmation of the whole book is that in Jesus the truth of God is known,—" He that hath seen Me hath seen the Father " (xiv. 9) : " To this end have I been born, and to this end am I come into the world, that I should bear witness to the truth " (xviii. 37). To receive this truth is to have eternal life (i. 12, 18, 49 ; iii. 16, 33–36 ; iv. 26 ; v. 24, 39 ; vi. 40, 68 ; viii. 28, 31, 32 ; xi. 25 ; xii. 44 ; xiv. 9 ; xv. 23 ; xvii. 3, 6, 14, etc.). Thus the message of the Fourth Gospel is that, because of all that Jesus did and was, His thought of God may be ours. It is summarized in the closing words of the prayer of chapter xvii., " O righteous Father, the world knew Thee not, but I knew Thee ; and

these knew that Thou didst send Me ; and I made
known unto them Thy name, and will make it known ;
that the love wherewith Thou lovedst Me may be in
them, and I in them."

(II) THE JOHANNINE EPISTLES.

The Johannine Epistles are closely related, both in
style and thought, to the Fourth Gospel, but the
difference, whether it be of authorship or purpose, is
sufficient to need separate treatment.

The writer is very emphatic as to what it is that
saves and transforms a man. To express this he
does not need to speak of the death of Jesus,—" Whosoever believeth that Jesus is the Christ is begotten
of God " (v. 1) : " Whosoever shall confess that
Jesus is the Son of God, God abideth in him "
(iv. 15). These statements define the writer's meaning
when he uses more general phrases, such as, " This
is His commandment, that we should believe in the
name of His Son Jesus Christ " (iii. 23) : " These
things have I written unto you, that ye may know
that ye have eternal life, even unto you that believe
on the name of the Son of God " (v. 13).

What the writer holds to be the significance of
believing in Jesus as the Christ or Son of God is made
clear both at the beginning and end of the tract. It
is that in Jesus we so know the truth of God that
we are brought into fellowship with God. In
i. 1–4 we are told that in Jesus the Word of Life was
so manifested as to give men " fellowship with the
Father." In i. 7 ff. it is repeated that Jesus so
reveals God that an honest response to His truth
brings men into fellowship with God,—" This is the
message which we have heard from Him and announce
unto you, that God is light. . . . If we walk in the
light, . . . we have fellowship one with another." The

substance of this message is again repeated at the close of the Epistle,—" And we know that the Son of God is come, and hath given us an understanding, that we know Him that is true, and we are in Him that is true, even in His Son Jesus Christ. This is the true God and eternal life " (v. 20).

It is within the scope of this Gospel that we find, as part of it, the statement that " the blood of Jesus His Son cleanseth us from all sin " (i. 7). But the sequel of these words makes it clear that by " cleansing " the writer does not mean justification or even forgiveness but actual liberation from sin. For he goes on, " If we confess our sins, He is faithful and just to forgive us our sins, and to cleanse us from all unrighteousness," thus making confession the condition of forgiveness and distinguishing forgiveness from the cleansing which he has just attributed to " the blood of Jesus." He evidently, therefore, has in mind the moral and spiritual power of the death of Jesus in overcoming sin rather than the idea that His death was a necessary preliminary to forgiveness. His thought with regard to forgiveness thus agrees with the teaching of Jesus and contradicts the assumption of the traditional gospel. When he writes, " He that saith he is in the light and hateth his brother, is in the darkness even until now. He that loveth his brother abideth in the light " (ii. 9, 10), he is putting into other words the reiterated saying of Jesus that if we forgive others God forgives us.

It may perhaps be contended that the traditional gospel finds support in " your sins are forgiven you for His name's sake " (ii. 12). But the context leaves it uncertain whether " His " refers to Jesus or God, the verses following making the latter more probable. And the expression " forgiven for His name's sake " is a paraphrase of " He is faithful and righteous to forgive us our sins " (i. 9) where it is God that is spoken of.

The writer states Jesus' relationship to sin in terms that are not confined to His death but include His whole life,—" He was manifested to take away sins " (iii. 5) : " To this end was the Son of God manifested, that He might destroy the works of the devil " (iii. 8). And when he uses the term " propitiation " he applies it to the life of Jesus as a whole,—" Herein was the love of God manifested in our case, that God hath sent His only begotten Son into the world, that we might live through Him. Herein is love, not that we loved God, but that He loved us, and sent His Son to be the propitiation for our sins " (iv. 9, 10). It is thus Jesus Himself rather than His death that is the propitiation. So too in ii. 2 : " Jesus Christ is the propitiation for our sins ; and not for ours only, but also for the whole world." And in iv. 9, 10 we learn what the writer means by " propitiation." It is simply that which assures us that God's love is so great that even our sin cannot cancel it : he uses it as a figure for the truth that " hereby know we love, because He laid down His life for us " (iii. 16).

(12) THE EPISTLE OF JAMES AND THE SECOND EPISTLE OF PETER.

These two books add little of a positive nature as to the gospel of the early Church, but they give us two interesting glimpses of its attitude to the teaching of Paul.

2 Peter is seldom regarded as genuinely apostolic and is generally dated amongst the latest books of the New Testament. The writer warns the Church against the danger of misunderstanding the epistles of " our beloved brother Paul," " wherein are some things hard to be understood, which the ignorant

and unsteadfast wrest, as they do also other scriptures, unto their own destruction " (iii. 15, 16). These words suggest that the writer saw in the Church a tendency towards an undesirable development of Pauline doctrine. Together with this warning we note that in his description of the Church's heritage in Jesus (i. 1–11) he makes no use of either the ideas or terms in which Paul approximates to the traditional gospel.

In the Epistle of James we have another teacher of the early Church who found difficulties in certain elements of Paul's teaching. For there is little doubt that in what he says about justification by faith (ii. 14–26) James has the doctrine of Paul in mind either as it appears in his letters or possibly as it was held in an exaggerated form by some section of the Church. And it is interesting to note that what he condemns is precisely that element of Paulinism to which the traditional gospel appeals. This accords with the fact that no other book of the New Testament comes so near in thought to the teaching of Jesus as recorded in the first three Gospels.

(13)

This very cursory survey of the books of the New Testament shows us that in essence their gospel has a far stronger likeness to the gospel that Jesus preached than to the traditional gospel : it was the gospel of God known in the love and life and death of Jesus. Phrases and figures that can be interpreted in support of the traditional gospel are comparatively seldom used ; and when they are found, a balanced assessment of the writer's thought always convinces us that they are not a simple and direct expression of his experience of Christ.

It may be said, How then do you explain the

existence of the traditional gospel ? Now we have
already seen that certain elements of thought in the
early Church tended in that direction. So that the
question is, What ultimately gave these tendencies a
dominance that they did not have in apostolic times ?
And it is not difficult to point to a factor quite
capable of this result, though other factors co-operated,
such as eastern dualism with its recognition of the
devil's rights over mankind and Western legalistic
ideas of God's relationship to man. The traditional
gospel of the Church has always had as its background, or rather as its base, the doctrine of everlasting torment. To which it may be retorted that
the New Testament writers had the same doctrine.
That, of course, is open to dispute : the passages
generally appealed to are very few in number and
do not necessarily support the conclusion. But in
any case this is indubitable,—that nowhere in the
New Testament do we find the possibility of eternal
future misery enforced as a motive for accepting the
gospel in the way in which in subsequent ages it has
been used to urge men to accept the traditional gospel.

The belief in the endlessness and aimlessness of
future punishment introduced a strongly unethical
element into the idea of God's relationship to man
just where man's salvation was concerned. Hence
came the logical impossibility of retaining a purely
ethical and spiritual idea of salvation.

8

CHAPTER IV

EXPERIENCE

(1)

FORGIVENESS of sins involves the religious side of a moral experience. The sense of sin, which cries for forgiveness, is the consciousness of wrong-doing when God is taken into account : it is moral self-condemnation made explicit and reinforced by being brought into relation with what man conceives to be the ultimate truth of life. It is not an external addition, but is rather the development of moral self-condemnation into greater intelligibility and more permanent effectiveness.

For if moral self-condemnation is to be anything but a vague and passing uneasiness it must be seen in its relationship to our dominant ideas of life. The mental pain of self-blame always compels us to a certain amount of thought. We recognize that we did something that we knew to be wrong and something that we need not have done ; for if we can persuade ourselves that we acted in ignorance, or that no other course was open to us, we exonerate ourselves. If we cannot thus exonerate ourselves, the massive though vague pain of regret generally makes us resolve not to repeat the wrong action. But if thought goes no farther than this, then the resolution has little behind it but a fluctuating feeling. The very circumstances under which temptation recurs will be those that capture the attention and make us forget the pain of our regret. So that in common human experience, despite moral self-condemnation, it is generally easier to do wrong the second time.

Self-condemnation is fruitful of good only when it is something more than our condemnation of one of our past acts. It must be the condemnation of the self from which this act proceeds. It is not enough to resolve that we will avoid the repetition of a certain act : there must be a present realignment of the whole of life's interests so as permanently to avoid the level on which we succumbed to temptation. This involves a change of the ideas by which we live. For instance, one of the sharpest elements of regret is that our wrong-doing has hurt our fellows ; but thought quickly shows us that if we live from a self-preferent standpoint, our life will find its inevitable issue in such actions : we can securely avoid them only by living from a different point of view,—which involves a different philosophy of life. Moral self-condemnation is thus not likely to be lastingly effective unless it brings us to see ourselves in the light of a larger and deeper idea of life than that by which we have hitherto lived. But in so doing we pass beyond the sphere of the purely moral to the philosophy or religion of life.

If a man's interpretation of life is religious, the strength and quality of his sense of sin will depend upon two factors,—his fear of punishment at the hands of God and his estimate of the character of God.

In the earlier stages of moral development, fear of punishment may serve as a temporary expedient in the acquisition of self-control. It is capable also of freeing the soul from bondage to the delights of the lower sorts of selfishness. But the appeal of fear is not in itself a moral one. It may induce conformity of act without increasing love of right ; while to certain fiery souls threat of punishment is rather provocative than deterrent. In our fear of punishment at the hands of God, the only morally redemptive element is in the recognition and feeling that we deserve it. But the extent to which we feel we deserve punishment from God depends upon our estimate of His character and of His interest in the humanity (including ourselves) which we have wronged.

The dominant element in any wholesome sense of sin must therefore be the character of God and not fear of His stroke. If fear predominates, it argues something wrong with our idea of God's character, which will be found to react badly on our moral self-judgment. Especially is it so when the divine penalty is thought of as exceeding all that is ever deemed humanly just. An example of this is to be found in *Grace Abounding*, in which we have the history of a soul racked by the fear of hell. The sins of which Bunyan accuses himself are bell-ringing, dancing, swearing and lying. It is significant that there is no mention of malice, anger or cheating, which are usually the serious elements in swearing and lying. This suggests that the latter were probably no more than the thoughtless and possibly not inartistic indulgence of the extraordinary powers of imagination and language which afterwards gave *The Pilgrim's Progress* to the world. There is also no mention of the pride and selfishness and cowardice that are in every unbiased self-condemnation.

But when fear of punishment diminishes to a right proportion, a lively sense of sin is found to depend entirely upon a lively sense of God's goodness. And then it is that we have a wholesome and effective religious interpretation and reinforcement of moral self-condemnation.

Apart from fear of punishment, a sense of sin can

thus come only when we believe that the ultimate truth as to wrong-doing is that it foils God's purpose and afflicts His love. In this case belief in the love of God must precede a sense of sin. We have seen (p. 66) that with Paul the sense of sin followed rather than preceded his conversion, and his conversion was his acceptance of Jesus as Lord and Christ, i.e. as the exponent of God's will and character. To the evidence already considered we may add an examination of the tenses of Rom. vii. 7–25. Where he uses the past tense (7–13) there is no indication of a sense of sin but only the retrospective statement that he had sinned. Where a sense of sin is expressed (14–25) the tense is vividly present. It is difficult, especially in view of the close of this passage (v. 25*b*) to understand it in any other sense than as describing Paul's experience at the time of writing. It may perhaps be said that Paul at his conversion had a subconscious sense of sin, but this is to play with words, for to have a sense of sin is to be conscious of one's self as a sinner.

We have the same order of experience in 1 John i. 5–10, where cleansing from sin by the blood of Christ is made a sequel of walking in the light, i.e. of honestly accepting the truth that Jesus reveals of God. The suggestion is that only in the light of God as revealed in Jesus do we know ourselves to be sinners.

It will probably seem to many people a paradox and a contradiction of experience to say that a true sense of sin follows rather than precedes the acceptance of Jesus' revelation of God. But their difficulty will be seen to arise partly through confusing moral self-condemnation with a sense of sin and partly through regarding the sense of sin as mainly fear of punishment. The distinction between moral self-condemnation and the sense of sin has already been noted. Moral self-condemnation is the painful recollection that we have voluntarily done what we knew to be wrong. As such it is the necessary prerequisite to a redemptive understanding and acceptance of Jesus' truth. But as such it is not yet a sense of sin, for there may be genuine self-blame without any belief in God at all, so that the theological distinction between moral self-condemnation and sense of sin is justified, sense of sin being the religious development of moral self-condemnation.

But the experience of moral self-condemnation may have various sequels. We may repress the painful remembrance and divert attention to more agreeable interests. Or we may make the often unfulfilled resolve not to repeat the offence. The third possibility, as we have seen, is to recognize that we did wrong because we were wrong, i.e. because the whole attitude and trend of life was amiss. This sets us to seek a truer base for life and so brings us to the realm of religion. And here the quest takes the form of the question, What is man to God? or rather, since we did not ask this question soon enough, it must now be asked in the more difficult and anxious form, What are sin and the sinner to God? And our sense of sin is our consciousness of moral wrong-doing as affected by our answer to this question.

Now so long as God is thought of as mainly and supremely the punisher of sin, there can be a very acute sense of sin without any experience of His love as it is revealed in the cross of Christ. But two things must here be remarked. In the first place, the God we know in Jesus Christ is not supremely the punisher of sin, so that if we engender a sense of sin by the belief that He is so, then we are to that extent unable to understand His revelation in Jesus.

The second thing is that, as we have seen, unless
fear of God's punishment is secondary to the moral
appeal of His character, our sense of sin will be rather
a perversion than a fulfilment of our moral self-blame.
If it is to be thoroughly helpful, our sense of sin must
come rather from what we believe about the character
of Him who punishes than from the expected penalty.
And this brings the question, Why does God punish ?
To answer that He punishes sin because He loves
mankind is to say what becomes intelligible and
credible only in " the word of the cross," for it is
only there that we see in God a love great enough
to suffer ; and to punish for love's sake is to suffer
for love's sake.   Short of this,—and all answers that
make a sense of sin precede our knowledge of the
love of God in Christ must come short of this,—there
is no morally redemptive answer to the question,
Why does God punish sin ?   Indeed, we might say
that short of this there is no answer that does not
confuse our moral life, just in so far as it is taken
seriously.   To say that God must punish sin because
He is righteous is not an answer but an evasion of
the question.   All it does is to state dogmatically
that the law that sin must be punished is an essential,
if not the essential, law of righteousness, and at the
same time to suggest that God obeys it rather from
necessity than desire.   It masks the question why
He wills that righteousness should punish sin.   Why
then is sin an offence to Him ?   How does it hurt
Him ?   And if we answer that it hurts Him because
it hurts His children, we are again speaking of a love
that suffers.   All other answers, as that it is rebellion
or an affront to His majesty, suggest that He acts
from the sort of self-love that our moral consciousness
condemns.   And such answers can obviously bring
no real help to the experience of moral self-condemna-

tion. At best it revolts against them and is thrown back upon itself : at worst they quash its problem by non-moral considerations.

We thus see that moral self-condemnation is not a sense of sin, since there may be no thought of God in it ; and that, being a concomitant of all honest moral experience, it is essential to an honest acceptance of the truth of Jesus. But we also see that if the sense of sin is created by any other thought of God than that He loves, it blunts and confuses the moral elements of self-blame. Moral self-condemnation does not find its true religious interpretation except in the suffering love of God : therefore it is that a wholesome sense of sin follows the acceptance of the truth of God as it is in Christ. The experience of release from the sense of sin through faith in the death of Jesus finds its ultimate explanation in the fact that the truth of Jesus destroys the power of lower ideas of God and so removes such sense of sin as attends them. The work of Jesus is not to remove the sense of sin but to replace a wrong one by a wholesome and quickening one.

It is therefore useless to expect a sense of sin unless we have a strong conviction of the goodness of God. And it is precisely this that the world to-day lacks. So that before any gospel of the forgiveness of sins can have power or meaning for the world, there must be a prior gospel that puts within the reach of men a strong belief in a God of love. And such a gospel might well be described as an assurance that for them " the kingship of God is at hand," for only by their knowledge of God's love can His kingship in their hearts be so effective that they feel their wrong-doing to be a hurt to God.

Insistence on the traditional gospel has obscured the existence and power of this broader gospel that

Jesus Himself preached. But Jesus' gospel remains
as an eternal possibility for mankind. An honest
and simple contemplation of the life, the acts and
words, the suffering and death of Jesus makes the
God of Jesus credible to us : it does more,—it
makes it impossible not to believe in Him. That, at
least, is the experience of the writer. After much
endeavour for an adequate sense of sin and for an
understanding and experience of forgiveness that
should be the ground and beginning of a true life in
God,—an endeavour which was continually frustrated
by the haunting lack of sure belief in any God to
sin against or in a love of God great enough to make
sin against Him more than formal,—he found that,
in contemplating Jesus, God and God's love became
momentarily real and moving. And slowly came the
conclusion and conviction that here was the true
beginning and the effective gospel. It could be no
accident that God was burningly real to him only
while his thought was set upon Jesus. This was the
very gospel that Jesus preached and for which He
laid down His life.

It may perhaps be said that this was not the gospel
of Jesus, for though it may be granted that His
gospel brought a higher idea of God, yet He did not
bring belief in God, for the Jews already had it.
This is no doubt true. But it may be pointed out
that one effect of Jesus' teaching has been so to lift
the moral ideal of the world as to discredit all ideas
of God lower than that which He taught, with the
result that apart from Him no belief in God is possible.
In any case the writer's experience was that apart
from Jesus the utmost that conviction could achieve
was to reject the denial of God's existence, to enthrone
" the grand Perhaps " in varying degrees of probability, to achieve a departmental belief but not a

whole-hearted assurance. He could feel that denial of God was moral diffidence, could find God intellectually credible, but could not take the belief to heart. This experience needs a little further analysis.

When we are endeavouring to think of God we are endeavouring to find the fundamental truth of life, the reality underlying all things. It is clear, therefore, that we must seek Him in that of which we are most sure. Now of all the things of which the writer was sure, he found only one that meant anything in this quest. All the rest seemed to justify the saying that what can be proved is not worth the proving : nor could this one be exactly proved : it seemed rather to be given with conscious life. He was sure of a direction in his life independent of that which his life actually took. He was absolutely sure that he was not what he ought to be, and no endeavour could make him think that he was, or that this unfollowed direction was a mental fiction. Whatever might be the way he actually took, he was absolutely sure that the way of kindness and justice and truth was the way proper to his being and that in taking other ways he was " going out of acquaintance with himself."

And in this absolute assurance that action in a certain spirit befitted him, he saw a declaration as to the nature of the universe from which he had derived his being. If there was a right way for him, whether he took it or not, the roots of that rightness must be found in the very nature of things, in the constitution of the universe that gave him life and all life's qualities. He is sure that he is not speaking nonsense when he says that he was meant to be other than he has been. Even in wrong-doing the assurance persists that there is a difference between right and wrong, and the right is still known to be more consonant with reality than is the wrong. And there seems no way of thinking intelligibly of this sense of direction except by seeing in it a declaration of a good purpose in the universe, which is tantamount to finding in it the voice of a Purposer. Such a conclusion seemed only to make explicit what was implied in that of which he was so sure.

But his experience was that although he was sure of a direction in life other than any direction of his own creating, and though God and God's goodness seemed implied in this assurance, yet when he tried to make the logically resultant faith explicit it had very little vitality. The reason of this must be somewhat as follows.

When what is implied in the sense of direction in life is made explicit and becomes a professed belief in a good God, it comes into contact and comparison with all the other ideas accepted by the mind. Every statement claiming to be true is tested by what is already accepted as fact or truth. But the idea of a good God, i.e. of a good will that in some sense dominates the universe, is, more than any other idea, compelled to make itself good in face of all the facts of the universe. But I have to confess that this good will does not dominate me. In every act in which I have been false to my sense of the right way, I have established in the universe a fact that is incompatible with the dominance of a good purpose there, and the incompatibility is felt as soon as the belief in a good God is made explicit. By wrong living I have created a self that is incompatible and incongruous with what is implied in my knowledge of right. So that either the fact of my wrong-doing disproves God and His goodness, or in doing wrong I have so committed myself to self-contradiction and unreality that to me the real appears unreal. In any case my belief in God becomes faint and formal and ineffective.

And it should be noted that this faith-quelling incongruity arises not so much from the memory of separate and past acts of wrong-doing as from the consciousness that the goodness of God, as implied in my sense of right, is not effectively dominant in my life as a whole. Even in the moments where I think specially of it, I do not find that I give it whole-hearted loyalty. It is a goodness that has more authority than power : it is king in the logic of my morality but is not effectively regnant in my affections and acts. And the reason of this is not hard to detect. The goodness of God as implied in my moral con-sciousness is of too mediocre a quality to command all my being. It is correct, but not heroic. It is adequate to rebuke but not to attract. It compels my assent but it does not fire my enthusiasm. It is a hand that points to the goal with a persistence indifferent to my wandering, not a hand that invites or reaches after me with anything like the urgency of human love. The idea of the goodness of God so found has low credibility because the goodness itself is not intense enough. My wrongness makes God's goodness incredible until I can find that which shows His goodness to be of the redemptive sort, pure and intense enough to overcome evil, until I can find in Him a love so entire as to take the unfeigned loyalty of all my being.

And it is precisely this, which I cannot find in myself, that I find in Jesus. I see in Him a man who at the base of His being has, as all men have, a sense of direction that speaks of a good purpose in the universe. But I see in Him one in whom the goodness of God, revealed in this way, is of such a quality that it has power to triumph, who so thinks

of God as to love God with all His being, who thus
in all acts is true to His inmost thought. Whether it
was His truth of God that enabled Him to be what
He was, or whether it was what He was that gave
Him His thought of God, is perhaps a useless inquiry :
the fact remains that His truth of God dominated
His life, and that the goodness of God shown in Him
was of the self-giving, invasive, redeeming sort that
has triumphant power over the human heart. He
who accepts Jesus' thought of God finds a God whom
he cannot but love. He is thus drawn back from
the desires and activities that deny the goodness of
God, so that the things that make God unreal to
him are removed from his life, or rather he is drawn
towards a realm of reality whose centre is God. The
God of Jesus does actually dominate the heart that
learns to know God in Him, so that the difficulty of
believing in the dominance of such goodness in the
universe is overcome.[1]

And it is Jesus Himself that makes His thought of
God credible to us. It is a fact of experience that
while my mind is set upon Jesus, I find that I cannot
but believe in His God and Father. I am then as
sure of the Heavenly Father made explicit in His life
as I am of the sense of direction in my own. And
these two assurances are one, for the significance of
Jesus lies in His relationship to my sense of right. I

[1] The experience here described has some analogy to that which
lies behind Paul's language in the Epistle to the Romans. The
sense of direction in the human conscience interpreted as a revelation of God is roughly equivalent to the Pauline idea of the law
(cf. Rom. ii. 14, 15). And Paul found the law weak because it
was only a partial revelation of God. The righteousness of God
revealed in it was not commanding enough to secure man's whole-
hearted loyalty. "The law of sin and death" appealed to fear
or hope of reward and therefore did not lay hold of the highest
in man. But Paul found in Jesus a higher sort of righteousness
revealed as God's (Rom. i. 17). Through Christ he found in God
a love that "constrained" effectively, that made him "more than
conqueror."

see in Him what I cannot doubt to be the quality of life towards which my sense of life's direction points. This is a matter deeper than conclusion from observed premises : it is bound up with the only terms on which self-conscious life can function. Unless we are prepared to obliterate the difference between right and wrong, and with it the specific quality of self-conscious activity, we cannot but believe that the right is nearer to the ultimate reality than is the wrong. We cannot but confess that Jesus is more right than any that we can set beside Him and therefore more in harmony with the truth of things.

And in this experience it is the suffering and death of Jesus that give final power to the gospel of His life. The contemplation of the cross, more than all else, quickens faith in God and makes His love a penetrating and transforming reality. And why this should be is not hard to understand. The contemplation of suffering has a peculiar power to move our hearts and make us think, but this is only part of the reason. When a man follows truth to suffering and ignominy and death, we have the surest token that truth is dearer to him than all else. And failure is of all things the most profound revealer of the depths of the heart. The cross not only sets the final seal of complete sincerity to what went before, but opens to our eyes a depth and utterness of self-devotion that neither word nor act could reveal. It is the crucified and heart-broken Jesus that is the power of God because

The nobleness of love comes in love's woe.[1]

But it is only when suffering follows act or attempt, and is seen in the light they give, that it reveals more than they do. Though failure reveals the heart's

[1] Masefield, *The Daffodil Fields.*

inmost in a way that success cannot, the whole meaning of its revelation depends upon the nature of the attempt that failed. In His death and suffering Jesus makes us sure of God's love because in them the activity and intent of His whole life culminate. In them His life's inmost truth and motive come most indubitably and strongly to light, so that they arm God's love with its proper power.

The assurance of God that thus comes to us through Jesus is not the sort of assurance that can be obtained by logical deduction from observed facts. It is the bringing to explicitness of an assumption which we make in all moral action. When we are convinced that " this ought not to be," we feel that the very nature of the universe is behind the judgment and are sure that in this assumption we are not altogether befooled. It is the faith implied in this assumption that is brought by Jesus to know itself and is thus made unashamed and able to take the field promisingly in conscious life. With the validity of this assumption we shall deal in another chapter.

(2)

It is hardly needful to ask what boon such a gospel brings to life. To be able to believe heartily that God is such as Jesus showed Him is in itself the supreme boon. But it is as well to compare it with the blessings offered by the traditional gospel.

The great boon of the traditional gospel is the assurance of individual well-being in the future world. Its appeal is thus chiefly to self-regarding motives, and therefore it does not make directly for unselfish living. And in so far as its centre of gravity is in the hereafter, it tends to diminish concern for the betterment of this world. Those who have any sort of contact with Jesus always catch something of His spirit of helpfulness to mankind, and it is undoubtedly so with the adherents of the traditional gospel, but this happens rather in spite of than by means of their idea of the gospel.

There can be no doubt that, throughout all the centuries in which the traditional gospel has been preached, the power of the truth of Jesus to remake the world has been disastrously handicapped by the emphasis put upon self-safety in the hereafter. We see this in the anchorite who left society to itself that he might save his soul ; we see it in the mediæval Church with its ideal of the ascetic celibate to whom the common values and affections of life were a temptation of the devil : we see it in the more modern Protestants who acknowledged God's blessing in the security of their position both here and hereafter and approved a dispensation of providence that enriched the few at the expense of the many and so saved the many from the danger of being made careless of the next world through too great comfort in this. Whichever it be of these that we consider, we cannot wonder that the improvement of this world was slow under a gospel so framed as to deflect the pressure of the teaching and spirit of Jesus as far as possible from incidence upon the ways of this life.

On the other hand, the gospel that Jesus preached was the gospel of the kingship of God, which pointed directly, though not solely, to the shaping of this world to God's intention. The traditional gospel leads only indirectly, or rather incidentally, to the enthronement of God in human conduct. In his argument on justification, in which Paul approaches nearest to the traditional gospel, he seems to have felt that the doctrine needed defence against the charge of leaving conduct unaffected (Rom. iii. 7, 8 ; vi. 1, 15), and he does not succeed in any very clear rebutment of the objection. But the man who finds in Jesus the truth of God cannot but desire, with an intensity commensurate with his belief, to enthrone God in all the inward and outward concerns of his own life and the life of the world.

The gospel that Jesus preached brings no private security to the soul that accepts it. The essence of its boon is that His thought of God becomes ours, so that once and for all it endues the universe in which we live with a dignity before which our own safety is a very little thing. It makes us know that the deepest reality of life is past our imagination wonderful and worshipful. It discovers in life an infinite worthiness. It convinces us of a God with whose love we do not want to bargain, of a Father from whose wrath we do not want to secure ourselves.

Life is no longer a wilderness between us and the promised land. We no longer merely tolerate the present world and make shift to get through it somehow, buoyed by the hope of a reversal of it all in the next world. Rather he who finds the truth of life in Jesus finds that the spiritual aspect of life is even greater and more wonderful than the physical. On the worth and wonder of the present he grounds his hope for the future. As Jesus Himself taught (Mark xii. 26, 27), belief in a future life has its ground in the reality of a present fellowship with God. And the man who knows God in Jesus makes no demand or stipulation for the future, but finds the ultimate reality to be of such a nature that he cannot but hope and believe.

(3)

It may perhaps be asked what, in this experience, becomes of the sense of sin.

It must be remembered that there are often elements in the sense of sin that are rather harmful than helpful to the spirit. We have already (p. 116) considered certain aspects of this, but there is another and more subtle danger that readily attends the attempt to cultivate a sense of sin. The disgusted contemplation of our ill deeds is often only the obverse of a desire to think well of ourselves. To make a duty of the sense of sin is to imply that we ought to be able to think well of ourselves, and thus it easily leads to self-satisfaction with our contrition. So that the deliberate cultivation of a sense of sin may result in the substitution of a specious humility for an honest fulfilment of duty.

For there is danger of confusion here. Sin, being the religious aspect of moral wrong, has always a double face, manward and Godward. Now, efficiency of life needs that our manward duties, so far as they call for definite acts, should be reasonably capable of discharge. To try to cultivate a sense of sin in respect to them may induce us either to offer the world contrition where it may reasonably expect fulfilment, or to adopt an impossible and therefore unwholesome standard.

But it may be truly said that the worth of the specific modes of conduct which we acknowledge as duties depends upon our love for our fellows, and that, since we never love them enough, we sin either in attempting too little, or at least in the spirit and motive of our attempts. Our fault is too much self-love, and we hate and despise ourselves for it. But self-hate and self-despising do not lead us to love others with an effective love. " Thou shalt love thy neighbour as thyself " reminds us of this. For, after all, we do in some sense represent humanity to ourselves, and contempt of ourselves is no more compatible with a right appreciation of others than is conceit of ourselves. Paul's advice is characteristically sane, " I say to every man that is among you not to think of himself more highly than he ought to think ; but so to think as to think soberly " (Rom. xii. 3).

The only wholesome remedy against our indurated self-love is to turn to the Godward side of the matter. Our lack of love to man is a sin against God's love. If, as Jesus has made possible for us, we feelingly apprehend in God a love that is wounded by our lovelessness, then our sense of sin is transformed into wonder at the goodness of God. To be able to forget ourselves in the enjoyment and service of God's love is the only solution of the problem of self-love :—

> We are wrong always when we think too much
> Of what we think or are : albeit our thoughts
> Be verily bitter as self-sacrifice,
> We're no less selfish.[1]

The love of God in Christ rids us of fear of punishment and relieves us of the task of trying to think well of ourselves ; and what is left of the sense of sin when these two are subtracted is sublimated into self-transcending wonder and work.

(4)

Since forgiveness of sins is intrinsically so important and is given so prominent a place in the traditional gospel, we must consider it in relation to the gospel as here understood.

To be forgiven by God, when it is no longer merely, or chiefly, exemption from everlasting torment, must mean at least two things. We must find in it both the assurance of a certain personal attitude of fellow-

[1] E. B. Browning, *Aurora Leigh.*

ship on God's part and the securing of our future against destruction by the effects of our wrong deeds and desires. These two needs are, of course, connected, and are, in fact, two sides of the same thing. For of the results of sin that threaten our future the chief is loss of fellowship with God, while, having that, we shall not find the rest fatal. Some of the so-called natural results of sin persist whether a man believes himself forgiven or not. Forgiveness does not restore wasted opportunities or cancel the mortgage of excess. And whether we distinguish or not (and we probably should not distinguish) between the results of sin and the punishment which God inflicts here or hereafter, a man must believe that what punishment God gives will be for his good, and he will therefore not desire to escape it.

With regard to the all-important thing—fellowship with God,—it is clear that there can be no fellowship between two if one wills good and the other wills evil. So that to repent, to turn from the wrong to the right, is the only efficient condition of forgiveness and restoration of fellowship: "If he repent . . . forgive him." But the difficulty is the fulfilling of this condition. The critical need is not the fellowship of God that we get when we have repented, but that fellowship with Him that we need in order that we may repent. And it is necessary to bear in mind that repentance is more than penitence. It is not only, and not necessarily, sorrow. It is change of mind, change of the direction of life.

There is a peculiar difficulty here. Of all the results of our wrong-doing the most abhorrent are those which fall in pain and degradation upon others. We hate ourselves for this and cannot but think that this self-hatred must echo the judgment of God whose children we have harmed and degraded. Yet to think that God is against us is to lose all hope of effective repentance.

For if we are to be able to repent, to turn from the evil to the good, certain conditions must exist. We must be able to think that our deeds are really ours, that they express our being and make us what we are, that they really matter, that when we do wrong it makes a difference to the universe and to God ; but we must also be able to think that in our self-condemnation and in our struggle for the better there is a real part of ourselves, and that God and the universe are the allies of this better self. We must be able to think that, despite our having sinned and despite our present sinfulness, God befriends us and holds to His ideal of us.

But this needs a far higher and more intense love in God than is implied in my own moral nature. In myself I know enough of God's goodness to know that wrong is a contravention of what the universe purposes. But if I know no more than this, I know only that my wrong-doing has made me an enemy of God. And to make repentance possible I need to know that God loves those who have made themselves His enemies. If He loves me, His love must be great enough to bear in pain the companionship of His indignation at my baseness.

But the assurance of such a love in God is precisely what I find in Jesus. He confirms the reality of human responsibility and of sin's contravention of Heaven's purposes. He makes me doubly sure of my sin's hatefulness to God because of its thwarting of His good purpose, and yet He assures me of a goodness in God so great that, in spite of all, God still values me, hopes for me, loves me. In Him this truth of God is so embodied that every time we think of Him our assurance and appreciation of God's love is deepened, our apprehension of His will is quickened, and our desire to do it grows stronger.

In producing this result both the life and death of Jesus are not only essential but mutually essential. Yet there is no doubt, as we have seen (pp. 126 f.), that in His suffering and death His power culminates and becomes finally effective.

It appears thus that the relation of the life and death of Jesus to the forgiveness of sin is that they give us the assurance of God's goodness which we need to make a real repentance (or change of mind) possible, and that when we repent God forgives. This brings us back to our starting-point. If we believe that God forgives those who repent, there is no problem of forgiveness, but rather one of repentance, and repentance depends directly upon an adequate knowledge of Him against whom we have sinned. And the gospel of Jesus is the gift of His thought of God to those who look upon Him honestly, to whom He thus " gives repentance " (Acts v. 31).

Nor is repentance limited to one crisis of conversion. It is a continual experience, as continual and powerful as the experience of God's fellowship. It is the path of spiritual progress, a daily approximation of our lives to the truth, an increasing loyalty to the ventures of the Spirit. And the fact that this is so will help to meet an objection that may be raised against the above account of repentance.

We have made the possibility of repentance depend upon the belief that our sin causes suffering to God, and it may be objected that this belief is by no means always prominent in the experience of repentance and is in any case a belief that is peculiarly difficult to hold in a vivid form.

The apparent justice of this criticism lies in the fact that the essential is not always the obvious.

The belief that God suffers for sin is undoubtedly difficult to hold vividly and is not always prominent in repentance. What is here contended for is that this belief (that God suffers for sin) is essentially involved in the beliefs that in Jesus we see the truth of God and that in His suffering we see the truth of God's relation to sin. And it is these latter beliefs that make repentance possible.

Repentance is made possible to us by the concrete whole of all that Jesus was. His teaching convicts : His manhood shames : in His hope we find hope : His suffering breaks the power of fear and pride : His love overcomes our selfishness and turns us to Himself. We submit to the power of these things and find new life in them. They are so moving, so convincingly true, that we do not stop to recognize that in giving them the place we do, we are tacitly taking the love and sorrow of Jesus to be the love and sorrow of God. And yet it is clear that the life and death of Jesus can help us to repentance only as He exhibits the truth of God, i.e. only as God's love was in His love and God's sorrow in His sorrow.

But another factor contributes to this difficulty. When our hearts are most deeply moved by the contemplation of the cross, we do for the time feel strongly the truth of God's sorrow for sin. But none can fully understand God's sorrow for sin unless he understands God's love. Only one who loved men as Jesus did could feel abidingly and strongly certain that God loves men to this extent. We can and must think that Jesus felt it, but it seems too high for us to attain to. In this respect we can say that the sufferings of Jesus were vicarious : He knew and entered into God's sorrow for sin as we cannot. And because He did this, we are gradually lifted into an approximation to His thought of God. Before we

may know God's sorrow as Jesus did, the love of
Jesus must create its own likeness in us.

While we are chiefly concerned about our own
repentance (and we have little call to be concerned
about the repentance of others while we are unrepentant), it is the human fact of Jesus that helps us.
We are moved chiefly by love of Him and of what we
see of God in Him. Not until we have learnt from
Him to love our fellow-men as He did can we have
His understanding of God's sorrow for man's sin.
The suffering of Jesus brings the sinner to repentance :
the sorrow of God makes the evangelist.

CHAPTER V

VALIDITY

(1)

To believe a thing is to be convinced that it is true. But when we come to think about our beliefs, we sometimes find that we can no longer hold them. To raise the question of the validity of a belief is to see how it stands this test of thought when applied to the utmost of our ability.

We must therefore ask, What can be said to show that the gospel, as here understood, is true. In answer we shall try to show that in all our moral activity there is implied a belief about life as a whole, that if we deny this belief our moral life becomes an absurdity, and that the gospel of Jesus is this belief in its truest and therefore most effective form.

This argument from ethical activity to the nature of reality is often parodied for the purpose of refutation as trying to prove that, because a thing ought to be, therefore it is. This is a shallow misunderstanding. Of course, some things that are ought to be, but the whole argument from what ought to be to what is depends upon the experience that many things that ought to be are not. Very commonly, and almost always where it is most significant, we use the word " ought " for what is not, or at least is not yet.

In discussing the relationship between our conviction as to what ought to be and our belief as to what is, the problem is commonly stated as that of the relationship between judgments of value and judgments of reality. This is apt to be misleading, for judgments of value are not always ethical judgments. " I want " is not the same as " I ought."

Of course, the simplest value-judgment has always a certain reference to reality. It tells us something about the universe. To say that I want a thing is to assert its value. This proves nothing as to the existence of the thing wanted. Yet it proves the existence of a want ; and the existence of a conscious want has a double significance for our notion of the nature of the universe. For the existence of conscious wants makes the question of the ultimate reality of the universe a very different one from what it would be were there no conscious wants in it. And since we generally try to get what we want and sometimes succeed, our conscious wants are an element in determining what shall be ; and that too is of great significance as to the nature of the universe.

But ethical judgments (with which we are here concerned) are not such simple expressions of want. It may be said that anything that has value is so far good, and that therefore the judgment, " This has value," is an ethical judgment. But to say this is to obscure the peculiarly concrete nature of ethical judgments. In general it is good for a man to enjoy music : in actual life it may be wrong for a man to enjoy music, for it may be that he ought to be doing something else. Actual ethical judgments always have regard to all the facts of the situation. They take peculiar account of concrete reality and of the whole of it, and are thus characteristically different from other value-judgments.

Thus, to say that I want something is to set a value on it and to utter a value-judgment. But to say that I ought to want it is to add an important element and to utter a value-judgment of a peculiar sort. And what is added contains a reference to reality, for the distinction of the things I ought to want from amongst the things I do want depends upon a conception of myself and my relation to the universe. And the validity of the distinction depends upon the validity of the conception.

What is implied in our moral affirmations must now be considered under its various aspects.

(2)

To say that a thing ought to be is to say that it is possible. We can never think ourselves under moral obligation to do the impossible, and the confidence with which I say, " I ought to do this," measures my confidence that it is possible for me to do it. And a judgment as to what is possible implies a judgment as to what is, for what is possible depends upon the nature of what actually is. When we say that a thing ought to be, we imply that we judge the universe to be of such sort that such a thing is possible in it. And we imply more than this.

For when we say that a thing ought to be, we do not mean that it will necessarily be. To say, " This ought to be," undoubtedly implies that it either may or may not actually come to be. That is to say that if the word " ought " has any valid place in our vocabulary and would not always be advantageously replaced by the simple future, " will," then in this universe all is not predetermined but there are real possibilities of alternative events. It would paralyse our moral life if we had to act on the assumption that whatever will be ought to be. But if it is granted that what ought to be is not necessarily what will be, then it involves the very important judgment that there are open alternatives in the universe.

This conviction is strongest when moral consciousness is most active. Conscious moral self-determination always involves the assumption that it is possible for us to do other than we determine to do. Luther's " I can none other " is sometimes cited against this, but surely this celebrated declaration simply meant that, as an honest man, Luther could take no other course : he would have been the last man to claim that it was impossible for him to be dishonest. Whatever a man may argue about moral freedom, he always, in all moral activity, assumes that he has it. As has been often pointed out, our praise or blame would on any other assumption be meaningless. It may perhaps be said, " We praise or blame a man, not because we believe him able to be other than existent factors make him, but in order that our praise and blame may be additional factors to determine his action." Yet we are aware that, if he knows that we praise or blame him for what we believe he could not help, our attitude will cease to have any moral influence over him. A thorough-going determinism thus assumes that the specifically ethical element of human intercourse is either an exhibition of our ignorance or an attempt to exploit the ignorance of others. And in such an atmosphere self-condemnation will rot into self-pity.

If we were convinced that more than one course of action was never possible to us, it would mean that the result of our apparent self-determination was on every occasion a foregone conclusion. We should in that case have to confess that all our consciousness of self-determination was illusive, for we should really be determined by factors preceding and independent of it. And if we come to this conclusion, it is difficult to see what use consciousness is at all. If it has no part in the determination of action, if it merely accompanies action without making any difference, why was it evolved and how has it survived and developed ? But if consciousness has any determining effect on action, we should surely expect to find it where we are conscious of determining. And we cannot be conscious of determining without assuming that there are alternative possibilities to be determined. It is only because the assumption of these possibilities implies so much with regard to the nature of the universe that their existence has ever been questioned. As it is, in order to save their theories men will deny in theory what they actually assume in every activity of their conscious life.

It is to be noted that moral consciousness does not claim " absolute freedom " (whatever that may mean), but only the existence of alternative possibilities of act. We may also conclude from the force with which science is invoked against the claim for such freedom, that it is moral activity alone that claims it. This suggests that apart from moral activity there would be no need to stipulate for possible alternatives and no occasion to question the universality of physical determination. So that if we grant the possibility of alternatives of act, the existence of the second alternative may be expected to be causally connected with the existence of the human moral consciousness. And this is corroborated by the nature of the choice as it appears to consciousness. For consciousness of choice appears as the possibility of either resisting or yielding, of either taking the initiative or letting things slide, of either putting forth effort to control passion or of yielding to it, of either determining ourselves or suffering ourselves to be determined by externals or antecedents or by those things within us that are not most intimate to consciousness. It seems as if conscious activity itself created the possibility of alternative act.

It is sometimes (e.g. E. Jones, *Papers on Psycho-Analysis*, edition 1918, pp. 94 ff.) taken for granted that the claim for moral freedom is the claim to be able to act without motive. It is then shown that when we think we have acted without motive, as in the arbitrary choice of a number, a motive was none the less present, but it was an unconscious one. And so it is argued that, since all acts that are not determined by conscious motives are determined by unconscious ones, the whole of our psychic life is strictly determined and therefore our so-called consciousness of freedom is only our ignorance of unconscious motive. But this whole argument is based on a misunderstanding of the claim for moral freedom. For to act without motive might be called " freedom," but it certainly would not be " moral." No experience that we call moral choice ever appears to us as unmotived liberty. Rather we are then most of all keenly conscious of the pressure of motives, only they are divided against themselves. We find ourselves, like Macbeth (Act I, Scene 7), or Hamlet (Act III, Scene 1), or his uncle (Act III, Scene 3), or Launcelot Gobbo (*Merchant of Venice*, Act II, Scene 2), drawn in opposite directions by two sets of motives. The solution does not come by calculation. Moral deliberation in the proper sense is not like business deliberation where by further thought or further data we are brought either to an inevitable conclusion or to such a nice balance of possibilities that we can toss for a decision. For moral choice is a choice of ends, not of means to an accepted end. The experience of moral choice is that the two opposed systems of motives which pull us in opposite directions are incommensurable. We cannot bring them together and judge them by an accepted standard, for their very difference is that they appeal to different standards. The only point of unity that consciousness finds in them is that they appeal to the same self. And it seems that what is at stake is the integrity of the self,—its ability to think of itself as an intelligible whole,—and that finally the self determines by determining whether to be active or passive, to yield or control, to enjoy the pangs of initiative or the sweets of inertia.

The psycho-analyst tells us that this conscious self-determination is really determination by unconscious motives. But if this is so, then consciousness at the height of its activity is utterly out of touch with fact. And it is difficult to see how consciousness, if this is the truth of it, can be anything but a constant source of error to the organism that possesses it. And this makes it hard to understand how self-conscious man has been victorious in the struggle for survival.

But, further, we are told that a striking characteristic of the unconscious is "its ruthless and absolute egocentricity" (op. cit., p. 632). So that if, when we think we are acting freely, we are really moved by an unconscious motive, we may also know that this unconscious motive is one of "ruthless and absolute egocentricity." Apply this theory to the case of a man who is wrestling with the temptation to save his skin at the expense of his friend and who, with what seems to him an agony of self-determination, clings to the nobler line of conduct. This theory of psychic determinism tells us that the man is deceived, for he had really no choice in the matter but was determined by a motive of which he was unconscious and therefore by a motive of "ruthless and absolute egocentricity."

(3)

There is another equally important matter in which the line of thought followed here may seem at issue with the conclusions or suggestions of certain psychologists. There is a tendency in psychology to-day to trace our sense of duty back to one or more instincts ; and it may be argued that it is therefore not to be taken as an indicator of the underlying reality of the universe. To which it must be answered that no psychologist has yet succeeded in giving a convincing and generally accepted theory of the derivation of the sense of moral obligation from the instincts (see p. 160) ; and that even if he had, it would not forbid us to find in our moral activity a key to the nature of the universe. For in order to give plausibility to the derivation of moral obligation from instinct we have to understand instinct so broadly as to make it inclusive of all vital conation. In this case, moral consciousness is life's activity grown conscious of itself, and not only conscious of itself but conscious of itself as a whole and of what is most important in itself. And this surely has some justification for being reckoned as an interpreter of life.

There is, however, reason for concluding that the sense of moral obligation cannot be derived from the instinctive, but that the characteristic and essential thing in it is the dominance of intelligence over instinct or at least the arbitration of intelligence between conflicting instincts.

There are, of course, large elements of the instinctive in all conscious activity, the instincts providing the raw material of moral choice. And we have to recognize that moral consciousness appears at a late stage of the race's development and that conduct at the earliest stages is dominated by instinct. And between these two is a stage at which it is difficult to distinguish the instinctive from the moral and which therefore gives a certain amount of colour to theories such as those which derive morality from the herd instinct or from the self-regarding instincts and sentiments. At a certain stage of human development the form of what was right to do was received by the individual from social tradition, and social pressure was at the same time a very great factor in impelling him to do it. The herd instinct was thus powerful in giving both form and sanction to conduct. At a somewhat later stage man's desire to think well of himself and to be thought well of supplemented the more directly social elements in supplying both form and motive for right action. But neither social tradition and pressure nor self-glory are to-day recognized as truly moral motives : we should condemn as morally worthless any life that was mainly guided and motived by these things. We count them, under such forms as self-righteousness and desire for popularity, to be amongst the most insidious and dangerous temptations.

On the other hand, it seems clear that the sense of oughtness is to be derived from (if it is not itself an aspect of) the unifying tendency of consciousness rather than from the instincts which are by themselves, in humanity at least, disparate, if not disintegrating forces. Whether the gratification of a particular instinct is right depends upon its relationship to the rest of life's interests. That information instinct itself does not and cannot supply. It is the proper work of intelligence, by which the instincts are compared and co-ordinated and which is itself the antithesis of instinct. Every instinct when stimulated tends to occupy consciousness and to unify it momentarily by the exclusion of other interests.

If this tendency is successful, the instinct passes into action and by so doing generally leaves the self another regret, an increased confusion, a deeper inward discord. In the actual struggle between right and wrong, as we are conscious of it, the stimulated instinct, which would reduce the intelligence to a means for its gratification, is pitted against the intelligence, which would delay gratification until all life's interests are brought into counsel and then, in view of the whole, would either permit or inhibit the progress of the instinct into action.

The survival and triumph of man in the struggle for existence was undoubtedly due to the excellent service which his intelligence gave to his instincts. But when one servant makes himself a vital necessity to many masters, it will not be very long before the positions are reversed and the servant controls the situation. When an instinct was stimulated, the thinking process was set a-going to discover ways and means towards gratification. And the very process of survey and search revived the recollection of other ends and so induced a conflict of instincts. There can be no considerable conflict of instincts unless the intellect is strong. The remembered interests must be remembered vividly if they are to compete with the stimulated instinct. The intellectual grasp of life as a whole must be firm if we are to see where and to what extent different instincts or interests are antagonistic. Intelligence thus brings about a conflict of the instincts, and in that conflict it alone can arbitrate. For it is clear that such a conflict of instincts can be wholesomely dealt with only from the point of view of a comprehensive and orderly idea of all life's interests. Thus the idea of what ought to be done, as contrasted with that which the roused instinct of the moment urges a man to do, is found, not in any other instinct, but in his most inclusive, fundamental and surest idea of himself. But a man's idea of himself is closely related to his idea of the universe in which he lives. Indeed, in the strictest sense, the two ideas are but different sides of the same idea. So that a judgment upon the self as a whole is involved in the judgment as to what ought to be done, and this judgment upon self as a whole involves a judgment upon the nature of the universe in which the self lives and from which the self has its being.

This judgment upon the nature of the universe which is implied in all moral judgment is precisely what is here contended to be the essence of religious faith. We shall return to this connection again, but in the meantime we need note one or two more points :—

(a) The large part that social tradition or the herd instinct played and still plays in our ideas of right is due partly to the individual's difficulty in discovering what is best for life as a whole. Over against his own brief, limited experience social tradition offers him the accumulated experience of the race tested in actual use. And then, too, his social environment is an enormously important factor in his universe, and proportionately affects his ideas both of the universe and of himself. But so long as man's action is unquestioning obedience to custom, it can hardly be called truly moral. The acceptance of this guidance is moral only when it is accepted because it is believed to be good. And we must bear in mind that on the lower levels of development most people take for granted the unique and supreme worth of their communities. They have also a notion that the well-being of their community depends on their conduct. On the other hand, as soon as growing intercommunication and intelligence bring men to think about their actions, moral judgment shakes itself free from social tradition and takes an independent though respectful attitude towards it. And the moral advance of the race in its higher stages has largely come through those who have dared to act in defiance of social tradition.

(b) It may be objected that if the idea of right is dependent upon the idea of self as a whole, then it is derived from the self-regarding instincts. But the self as a whole includes other instincts besides the self-regarding. And here we see the importance of recognizing that the idea of self as a whole implies the idea of the universe in which we live. For when we are thinking of ourselves in the narrower sense, i.e. when the self-regarding instincts are dominant, we lose sight of some of the most important elements of the self. We see the self as a whole only when we see it in all its relations to the world in which we live. In particular our love for others plays an essential part in our largest idea of self, which thus obviously transcends the self-regarding instincts. And if we try to find a motive for a right act in the desire to think well of ourselves, we see at once that we can think well of ourselves for doing a certain act only if we are persuaded that the act is worth doing in itself. But to say that a thing is worth doing in itself is tantamount to saying that it has value for the universe in which we live.

(c) The last conclusion becomes clearer if we consider what is involved in any wholesome reaction of intelligence upon instinct. Every instinct tends to fulfil itself in its characteristic act of producing certain results in life, and if intelligence has to judge between the instincts, it has to judge the value of these results. This involves a guess as to what nature is driving

at : it involves an attribution of ends to nature, and
a valuation of what appear to be nature's ends. An
intelligent control of the instincts must take count of,
and give place to, their function in the economy of
nature, and any attempt to harmonize them on any
other basis is to reckon without our host. So that
the attempt to order our instincts involves the adoption of a purpose in life by which we attempt to carry
on in our conscious acts the great process of nature,
and in so doing we are attributing a will and purpose
to the universe.

To this it may be objected that the above account
is mistaken, because the intelligence, in reacting
upon the instincts and attempting to harmonize
them, is merely serving the desire for as much
pleasure and as little pain as possible. In point of
fact this is partly, but only partly, true. It is an
alternative possibility in the intellect's control of
instinct, and we shall see that it describes the sort
of control that is wrong. A mother acts from love of
her children. If she ever thinks of justifying such
action to herself, it will probably be by telling herself
that it is right in the nature of things. We suspect
that, if she was told that at bottom she was moved
by nothing but the desire to get pleasure and avoid
pain for herself, she would either assume that her
informant was childless, or, if she accepted his statement, the theory would react unwholesomely upon
her ways. And this is what the modern psychologist, especially the psycho-analyst, sees. If we
want to live a whole and wholesome life, the instincts
must be dealt with in their natural setting and not as
means of pleasure and pain to the individual. The
psycho-analyst maintains that what he calls the
" pleasure-pain principle," i.e. action dominated by
fear of pain and love of pleasure, is precisely the

" infantile " and wrong method of dealing with
instinctive impulses. It leads to disordered and futile
mental life. Over against the " pleasure-pain principle " he sets the " reality principle," as the only
way to healthy and effective life, and in the " reality
principle " instincts are considered in the light of the
part they play in the whole concrete system of life.[1]

It is obvious, however, that considerations of
pleasure and pain do enter largely into our conscious
determinations. Instinct apparently sets intellect to
work by creating a feeling of discomfort, the pain of
which is therefore an important element in conscious
activity. And it would seem that when we con-
sciously determine our actions we must judge them
either in relation to the whole process of life or by
their power to produce pleasure and avoid pain.
And we must now consider this alternative.

(4)

Considerations of pain and pleasure are probably
factors in all volition. So far as they affect our
present inquiry, we can see that, in the intelligent
control of instinct, they must play their part in one or
other of two ways :—

It is possible for me to act on the axiom that my
pains and pleasures are more important to me than
the pains and pleasures of others. In this case the
pains and pleasures of others are important to me
only as, directly or indirectly, they affect mine. This
may happen through resulting action towards me or
through my sympathy with them or through other
means. But ultimately, on this axiom, my pleasures

---

[1] The psycho-analyst's insistence upon the necessity of the
" reality principle " for the right ordering of instinct and upon
the danger of perversion of instinct by the " pleasure-pain principle " may be compared with Paul's insistence (Rom. i. 18–32)
that the perversion of instinct may be traced to the neglect of a
right idea of God.

and pains are the only things that matter. Such a principle is quite intelligible, and may be applied to any situation that arises from the stimulation of instinctive tendencies through environment or otherwise.

But it is also quite possible for me to act on the axiom that my pleasures and pains are not intrinsically more important than the pleasures and pains of others. And there is no doubt that decisions are frequently made on this principle. It is capable of application to any situation in which the rivalry of instinctive tendencies calls for the arbitration of intelligence.

Here we have two principles of intelligent choice, both not only possible but both undeniably in actual use, both appealing to reason and feeling, both capable of being applied to the ordering of instinct, and yet they are mutually incommensurable, incompatible and antithetical. When we compare the two, we see that the former (in which my pleasures and pains are all-important) is intensely autistic, atomistic, subjective. It implies that the self is primarily a feeling being and only secondarily a thinker. Where act is determined on this principle the self rather yields to the pull of pleasure or is driven by the fear of pain than initiates its own course. Instead of determining, we allow ourselves to be determined. On the other hand, to act on the principle that others' pains and pleasures are as important as my own is to assert that it is proper to my being for my intellect to take precedence of my feeling. This difference describes with tolerable exactness what we experience in the choice between wrong and right. The right does appear to us as the impartial thing. And the effort to do the right,—that sense of effort which is our sense of self-determination,—does seem to lie in the refusal to be determined by considerations of our own pleasure and pain.

But when I act on the axiom that my pleasures and pains are of no more importance than those of others, it becomes obvious that some other criterion of value is involved than that of the amount of pleasure and pain. This axiom puts into other words Kant's principle that we ought never to use another person merely as an instrument but always also as an end in himself. We thus set a value on personality apart from any contribution that it makes to our well-being. But to say that a thing is of value in itself, i.e. apart from our valuation of it, or to say that it is an end in itself apart from our ends, is tantamount to saying that it is of value to the universe and is an end to the universe. In so doing we attribute to the universe a purpose and a sense of value, i.e. we find it dominated by a Will and Love.

It will now appear that the two principles of choice discussed here are respectively different aspects of those discussed in the last section. There we saw that the intelligent control of instinct was possible along two lines :—

(*a*) By viewing the instinct in its concrete wholeness as an element of the concrete whole of life, which involved the attribution of a purpose to nature, or

(*b*) By viewing the instinct from the point of view of possible pains and pleasures and by calculating the pains and pleasures involved in various possible courses of action.

Here we have seen that with regard to pleasures and pains two principles are possible :—

(*c*) The axiom that my own pains and pleasures are of more importance than those of others, and

(*d*) The axiom that my pains and pleasures are not intrinsically more important than those of others

,

which involves the attribution of ends and values to
the universe.

And it will be obvious that (*a*) and (*d*) coincide, as
do (*b*) and (*c*). In (*a*) and (*d*) both common sense
and the moral consciousness recognize the principle of
right action. And these—(*a*) and (*d*)—involve the
assumption that at the heart of the universe there is
something like a purpose and sense of value, and
that man's true life lies in fellowship and co-operation
with this Will of the universe.

It will also be noted that though both these pairs
of principles appear as methods for the intelligent
control of instinct, it is only in (*a*) (*d*) that the intelligence does control in the fullest sense. In (*b*) (*c*) the
self chooses as though it were dominantly feeling
rather than intellect and it chooses rather by yielding
than by exercise of effort. In (*a*) (*d*) the reverse is
the case; the decision is taken from the soul's most
commanding view-point and is carried out either by
dint of effort or with consciousness of power. This
comparison does not, of course, disparage the moral
value of emotion, without which there would be no
values of any sort. Rather there is a native affinity
between the impartiality of intellect and the self-
forgetfulness of love.

We can now bring the results of this and the last
section into comparison with those obtained when we
considered what was implied in moral freedom. We
saw that our moral nature repudiated the assertion
that nothing in the universe could be other than it is
and that everything is exactly determined by what
went before it. Our moral activity demands the
recognition that there are possibilities of choice. And
we saw reason to conclude that the second alternative
was supplied by the self-determining power itself.
In a universe that, to all appearances, is otherwise

physically determined, we found, where our experience is most intimate, that the thinking self is a determinant of events and can determine otherwise than physical causality would determine. And we saw the significance of this for our conception of the universe. In the present and last sections we have seen that the principle on which we act when we are using our fullest freedom and intelligence is one that involves the assumption that the universe is dominated by Thought and Will.

Another point must be noted. These two pairs of principles are those which lie respectively on either side of the moral alternative. The principle involved in our choice of the wrong is (b) (c) : the principle involved in our choice of the right is (a) (d). The (b) (c) principle regards the self as part of a physically determined universe : the (a) (d) principle regards the self as a thought-determined member of an intelligible and thought-dominated universe.

Leaving aside for the moment the consideration of any possible effect of conscious control, we see that the pressure of instinct upon us at any moment is what it is because of our heredity, history and environment. By physical inheritance we have certain instincts, and owing to their interplay amongst themselves and upon our environment, some particular instinct becomes predominantly active and gives rise in consciousness to the uneasiness of unsatisfied instinct and to the forecast of pleasures to be gained or pains to be avoided. The pressure of pleasure and pain upon consciousness (again leaving out of count for the moment any element of self-determination) is the impinging upon it of the universe as a system of physical causation. And the self would be merely part of that system if it were incapable of controlling such an instinct or could act upon no other principle than a calculation of the pleasures and pains involved. In the scheme of the determinist the universe as a physically causal system imposes control upon the individual consciousness either directly by a dominant instinct which is obeyed blindly or by the power of instinct to affect consciousness with pain and pleasure. On the other hand, if I endeavour to control instinct on any other principle than that my pains and pleasures are of all things most important, I can do so only by bringing the various acts of life into relation with a system of ideas of value and responsibility and obligation, of meaning and purpose. But, on the one hand, such a system cannot by any means be deduced from physical causation or from the physically conditioned pains and pleasures by which the outward universe affects consciousness. On the other hand, it involves not only the adoption of a dominant attitude and trend in my own life but the assumption of a purpose and meaning in the universe.

But here we have two rival conceptions of the universe,—on the one hand, as a system dominated by a good Will, on the other hand as a physically determined system. And although the latter, when presented as the whole truth is morally objectionable, it is too important scientifically to be disregarded. The necessities both of thought and action make it impossible to leave these two systems unrelated ; one therefore must be understood to include and underlie the other. If we make the physical primary, then the notion that the universe has meaning or purpose is a fallacy of the individual mind : self-determination is an illusion, for the possibility of alternatives of choice do not exist. In this case the one system explodes the other. And we have also the difficulty of finding any biological justification for the development of self-consciousness, since on this supposition it has no effect on action.

The alternative is to regard the physical system of the universe as the instrument and means of the dominating Will which our moral consciousness apprehends. In this case the one system includes the other, and it is possible to do justice to both. This solution is, of course, the affirmation of religious faith.

At this point the question arises, " If the physical is regarded as the expression of a divine Will, how comes it that the pressure of physical determination seems to clash with our self-determination for the good ? " The answer to which is that this opposition exists only so long as the universe is regarded as ultimately physical. So long as, and only so long as, we see in instinct nothing but a blind tug, or a power that drives us by pressure of pleasure or pain, we, thinking beings, are orphans and antagonists to the universe that bore us and encloses us. But when we believe that behind the physical is a Meaning and a Purpose of which we can apprehend enough to find a base for the intelligent handling of our lives, then the incompatibility disappears. Then the physical universe contributes its wonder and beauty to our thought of God, and in practice it is found to be sometimes a disciplinary and provocative resistance and sometimes a suggestion and helpful instrument conspiring with the inspiration of God.

It must not, of course, be thought that intelligent control never sanctions the dominant instinct of the moment. When it can do so, the man is at the top of his active power, and probably at these moments a finer efficiency of control is needed than when the instinct has to be held in check.

This discussion brings us to see that the resolution to do the right rather than the wrong is the claim to be a self and not a thing. It is the claim that our actions, and therefore ourselves, shall be shaped by our thought of the Whole rather than by the pressure of the immediately contiguous and surrounding frontier of the universe. The wrong, on the other hand, contains a self-contradiction, for in it we allow ourselves to be determined by the universe as though we were merely a fraction of itself, but our private account of our response to its pressures is that we serve our own pleasure only. In choosing the right we are preserved from self-contradiction by the voluntary adoption of what we conceive to be the purpose of the universe, and we do so by an act which asserts and establishes the claim to selfhood and is thus in a way creative. So that in our self-determination we have a creative and universal element like that which in a supreme sense we attribute to the dominant and underlying Mind and Will in which we find the ultimate reality of our universe.

(5)

We have now to consider more directly an aspect that has already been glanced at. We are sure that the right is the proper and befitting expression of our true selves, while the wrong is the reverse of this. What a man is convinced is right for him to do is thus inseparably connected with what he believes to be the fundamental truth about himself. Here then we have another important point of contact between judgments of value and judgments of reality, i.e. between our conviction as to what ought to be and our conviction as to what is. And we cannot deny this connection without disregarding one of the essential elements of moral consciousness. For man is absolutely sure that in choosing to do right he is

true to himself, and in choosing to do wrong he is
false to himself. He is sure that the right is consonant with the truth of his being, while the wrong
belies it.

But this belief about self carries with it a belief
about the universe. We see this when we face the
question, " If a man does wrong, he is a wrong-doer ;
how then can he think (as he certainly does) that to
do right is more proper to his true being than to do
wrong ? " For a man's idea of himself, as reflected
in what he believes he ought to do, does not depend
upon what he has actually done, but rests upon other
grounds. When we examine these other grounds
we find that they imply a strong, if vague, idea that
he was meant by the very nature of things to do
what he recognizes as the right. He feels that what
he calls duty is what the universe means him to do
and that to do the wrong is to put himself out of
joint with the trend and direction of the whole. We
see the justification of this notion when we consider
that a true idea of self must take into account the
relationships in which the self stands to the universe.
It must reflect all the self's concern with the universe,
i.e. all that the universe is to the self. The self draws
all its being and has all its qualities from the universe,
so that every judgment as to what fittingly expresses
the nature of the self is also a judgment upon the
nature of the universe. For instance, we are sure
that intelligence ought to dominate our activities
and that we ought not to let ourselves be driven
blindly by the force of instinct. But could this
assurance maintain itself in view of the derivation of
our being from the universe, if we were convinced
that intelligence did not dominate the universe ?
What *right* in that case would it have to dominate
us ? There might be convenience in its dominance,

but the word " right " would be inapplicable. We see, then, that to say, " It is right for me to do this," implies, " This deed expresses the nature of the universe." The assurance with which I make the first statement covers the second, and the validity of the first depends ultimately upon the truth of the second.

It must be borne in mind that these conclusions apply only to what in our moral activity we are sure of ; and we are absolutely sure only of the spirit in which we ought to act. In every concrete moral choice there are elements of which we are not sure. It is often right to act while we are still not quite sure about certain factors of our decision, though of course we must make as sure as circumstances permit. But we are always absolutely sure that it is right to act in the spirit of justice and truth and love.

This consideration will help to remove a difficulty. In different ages and in different countries men have thought different things right. And it is sometimes argued that the moral consciousness thus shows itself to be inconsistent and that therefore what is implied in it cannot be relied on as an interpretation of the universe. But it cannot be denied that all the higher development of humanity does agree upon the rightness of acting in the spirit of justice and kindness and truth. And on this level there is agreement that the spirit is the only element about which we are quite sure and that other elements in moral decision may be more or less uncertain. And when we find men absolutely certain about these other elements (except so far as certainty is justified on scientific grounds), we find that they are on the lower moral level, where morality has not quite emerged from mere custom. Their certainty is that of limitation and prejudice induced by suggestion and has no right to be considered as moral sureness in the specific sense.

And this last consideration answers those who reduce our ideas of right and wrong to results of social tradition and pressure. We must, of course, recognize the immense part played by social factors in the development of ideas as to what is right and wrong and also in supplying sanction, especially at the earlier stages. But we have to note that one of the characteristics of the true moral sureness is that it liberates a man in thought and act from the dominance of social suggestion and stress. The essential element of moral activity, therefore, is one that cannot be derived from these things.

We may note here that no theory that derives the sense of duty from any instinct or group of instincts can give a satisfactory account of its most remarkable characteristic, the absoluteness of its imperative. Instinct can be called absolute only when one instinct monopolizes consciousness ; but it is then a compulsive obsession and the subject is not morally responsible. Conscious moral control is made needful by the conflict of instincts, and no instinct or group of instincts has either absolute power or absolute right over other instincts. We have seen that the intellect, the growth of which brings the instincts into contact and conflict, is itself the only human activity that can settle their conflict. And it can do so effectively only on the assumption that it is wrong to sacrifice the interests of the self as a whole to the urgencies of a part. And in a conscious being the whole has absolute right over the part. But the task of defining the interest of the self as a whole cannot be the work of any one instinct or group of instincts, but is specifically the work of the intellect.

And to do this effectively the intelligence must be free from instinctive bias.

And we must here guard against the thought that, as the instincts form themselves into various groups, so the various groups may be thought of as forming the self by combining into one inclusive group. For there is no sense in speaking of a group of instincts unless we understand it to consist of two or more instincts that have come to work together instinctively. If we think of a conflict between the instincts that form a group, the group is dissolved. So that to consider the self as an inclusive group of instincts is to consider it before the conflict of instincts arises, i.e. before the self is in any sense moral and probably before we have any justification for using the term " self " at all.

We can therefore look upon the absoluteness of the moral imperative as the absolute right which, in the case of a conscious being, the whole has over the part. And we have seen that the idea of the self as a whole involves and reflects a similarly inclusive idea as to the nature of the universe from which the self derives its being. And here we have the justification of the common human conviction that the voice of duty is the voice of God.

It was one of Kant's great services to ethics that he made clear the absoluteness of the moral imperative. It is sometimes objected that his categorical imperative is void of contents and purely formal. But whatever may be true of the form in which he stated it, we have seen that we are always absolutely sure at least of the spirit in which we ought to act,—the spirit of justice and truth and kindness. And if, alongside this absolute element that characterizes moral activity, we place the undoubted fact that man's duty bears some relation to what he is, it becomes clear that an

11

absolute duty must be related to the whole of what he is and to the whole of the universe that makes him what he is. For a moral command which ignores any element of man's nature or of his universe cannot be more than hypothetical. The inclusion of the forgotten element may upset it. So that the characteristic absoluteness of the moral imperative is invalidated unless we see in it an implied judgment on the nature of the Whole of all being. And the implied judgment is that the ultimate reality of the universe is a Mind and Will, true, just and kind.

It may seem extravagant to claim that the moral consciousness of man reveals the otherwise unknown nature of the universe, but it seems clear that, unless we do so, we must recognize a radical and ineradicable contradiction at the heart of human life and a similar contradiction in the process of the universe. If there is no knowable purpose in the universe, then we have to acknowledge that where man is most convinced, he is most mistaken, that where he is most at pains to be right, he is most absurdly wrong. For man is sure that it is right to act in a certain spirit, and he is no less sure that the distinction between right and wrong has its roots in the nature of things. These two assurances are necessarily implied in each other, and they further imply that the right act expresses and carries out the purpose of the universe. If man is mistaken here, it is true that conscious control of life can remain, but it has lost its dignity. And with its dignity it has lost its use, for it can now be of use only as it contributes to pleasure, and there is no reason to think that man's life is more pleasurable than the wild life of smaller brains,—facts point to the contrary.

The intelligent control of action has undoubtedly been a powerful factor in enabling man to survive in the struggle of life. But unless intelligence can discover enough of the purpose of the universe to bring man into fellowship with the process that produced him, it must sooner or later defeat that process and become the evidence of its bankruptcy. For if man cannot apprehend in the process of the universe a purpose which he can value and adopt, then his conscious control of act must be based on a calculation of pleasures and pains. This is obvious when we remember that, so far as conscious control is concerned, the instinctive driving forces of life affect consciousness in only two ways, i.e. by the natural result at which the instinct drives, valued for its contribution to life as a whole, and by the incidental pains and pleasures. But to attempt to evaluate the things at which the instincts drive is to assume that nature is driving at some general goal. And if we deny that nature has a purpose, or that we can discover it, then we close this possibility and limit man's intelligent control of his acts to a calculation of pleasures and pains. But we have seen that to control instinct entirely from considerations of pain and pleasure is to become unwholesome and to pervert nature. For example, the conscious control of the sex instinct with the sole view of the pleasure of the individuals concerned does not produce good results for the race. Unless, therefore, there is in the universe a Mind that claims the co-operation of man's mind, we see that as man's mind develops it cannot but tend to defeat life. And yet mind seems to be the inevitable outcome of life, so that in this case life would be a tragic absurdity.

The cogency of this interpretation is perhaps best seen in the matter of truth. Our constant temptation is to believe what we would like to be true rather than what would approve itself as true to an impartial

judgment. And unless, by the endeavour to overcome the temptation, we get a more adequate repre-
sentation of reality, then the more honest our thinking
the further we are from the truth. But if the
endeavour for truth does bring us a better understanding of what really is, then the endeavour for
right, which involves, and may in one respect be
regarded as the endeavour for an understanding and
true estimate of life, must surely do the same. And
it may be expected to have an advantage in this
respect. For when we speak of seeking the truth, we
are generally thinking of the truth of some particular
matter, whereas our idea of the right turns upon our
idea of self and life and the universe as a whole. The
quest for the right is really the quest for the most
inclusive truth.

And here we may note the common assumption
that intellect, and not moral consciousness, is the judge
of reality. This distinction depends upon an artificial
abstraction of intellect from the concrete personality,
without which it is never found. It implies that
thought is a mere reflection of what is ; whereas the
mind that is not active reflects nothing, and in an
active mind its own activity is the most significant
element of reality. And the most significant aspect
of conscious activity is the self-judgment that speaks
in terms of what ought or ought not to be.

The assumption made by moral activity,—that there
is good purpose at the heart of the universe,—is in
some ways analogous to the assumption implied in the
conscious control of bodily movements—that there is
an external universe. It is possible theoretically to
question or deny the existence of an external world
and perhaps impossible to prove it. It is possible
for the body to move while the mind is dreaming,
But it is impossible for a man to exercise intelligent

and purposeful control of his body without assuming that there is an external world of which he has knowledge enough to make his actions worth while. And just as the conscious determination of bodily movement involves the assumption of the existence of an external world, so all moral self-determination involves the assumption that the difference between right and wrong has justification in the nature of reality, that rightness is nearer to reality than wrongness, as truth is nearer to it than untruth.

The difference between these two assumptions is due to the fact that the aspect of reality which we call the external world appears in consciousness with such vivid and aggressive detail. Our faith in it is so explicit, that only by dint of mental analysis do we come to own that it is after all an assumption and a faith, that it is something that could not possibly have entered into our minds through our sense organs, but is native to the mental processes that deal with what is thrust upon our senses.

On the other hand, the faith that is involved in moral activity has nothing to help it like the aggressive detail of the physical world. It is therefore likely to remain implied rather than to become explicit. And, as we shall see, there are peculiar difficulties to be overcome before it can be made explicit, the chief of which is that we cannot really believe that a good purpose dominates the universe unless it dominates us.

This last consideration is not likely to be challenged, but it has an interesting concomitant which needs to be noted. If we deny the moral consciousness the right to pronounce on the nature of reality, i.e. of God, it is because we have already assumed that we know the nature of reality to be not good or that we know the limits of our knowledge of reality and

know that we can never know it to be good. But
even in making these assumptions we are appealing
to the judgments of the moral consciousness, for
without it the word " good " has no meaning. If
goodness is dominant in reality, that truth can be
known only through the moral consciousness : if
goodness is not dominant there, only the moral consciousness has the right to say so.

But if goodness, being dominant in the universe,
is also to be dominant in man, he must have no other
ground than that of his moral consciousness for his
assurance of the dominance of goodness in the universe.
For if goodness is to be really supreme in man's heart,
he must commit himself to it because it is good,
not because it is revealed as a quality of a Being
on whom for other reasons he believes himself to
depend.   We can never make goodness supreme
within us so long as it comes to us first as the quality
of an Almighty Being.   It could never in this way
be supreme in its own right.   Goodness, if it is to be
really supreme in us, must not be imposed upon us
by an external reality.   Only when we enthrone it in
its own right does it discover to us the plenitude of
its sovereignty and become the mouthpiece of infinity.
We are sure that unless we do make goodness supreme
within us we are untrue to ourselves and to the reality
that bore us, and thus we find that to enthrone goodness in ourselves is to commit ourselves to the faith
that goodness is dominant in the universe.

(6)

We see, then, that all activity of the moral consciousness implies a judgment as to the nature of the
universe.   This judgment may be expressed in some
such statement as that the universe is dominated by
active Mind, i.e. by Will, the moral quality of which

is known in that which we are sure is morally right,—
the spirit of truth, justice, loving-kindness.

But it is one thing to be sure that something of
this sort is implied in moral activity; it is another
thing to convert this implication into an explicit
faith and to give it adequate expression. There are
thus two issues to the question of validity :—

(*a*) As to whether what is ultimately found to be
implied in the activities of the moral consciousness
may be regarded as a valid interpretation of reality.
This we have just discussed. At various specific
points we have seen that unless we accept as valid
what is implied in moral and conscious activity, the
whole process of conscious determination of thought
and act is discredited. And since in moral determinations conscious activity is surest of itself, it
follows that, unless we have there an approach to
reality, we cannot be sufficiently sure of anything in
the whole range of morality or religion to make them
worth discussing. It would mean that active thought
is essentially at issue with truth, that life can never
achieve any knowledge of itself. Man's only hope
then would lie in a retreat towards a less self-conscious and less intelligently critical form of life ; but
this would bring him to the level where all men at
all times have unhesitatingly believed in a God or
gods. If we refuse to accept what is implied in the
highest conscious activity of man, how can we accept
the criticism which the more highly developed men-
tality passes upon the religious affirmations of simpler
levels ?

(*b*) The second point appears when we ask what is
actually implied in moral activity. Can we give it
positive and explicit and valid expression ? This
is of immense practical importance. For the tendency of human development is towards more and

more intelligent control of itself, and if this attempt is to succeed, it will only be by making explicit what is implied in life. Here lies the chief difficulty and need of to-day, and it is here that Jesus meets our need.

In more primitive and less critical times many and various religious beliefs were possible. But intellectual and moral development makes it impossible for humanity to accept any but a supremely good God. The influence of Jesus has helped to discredit all conceptions of God lower than that which was embodied in, and accredited by, His life. For if our faith in a good God, as implied in moral act, is to be made explicit, our conception of God must be brought into relation with the whole of life's facts and accepted truths ; and all sub-Christian ideas of God are discovered to be inadequate both to moral and scientific experience.

For in all sub-Christian religions power has been the chief attribute of God, and goodness has never been more than secondary. But such a god cannot wholly command man's loyalty. Man can whole-heartedly give kingship only to one in whom goodness is supreme. A god to whom the pains of men are not as important as his own may appeal to man's self-concern but cannot take the whole homage of his heart. So that in the moral consciousness there is no true ground for belief in a god of this sort : it is not this sort of god that is there implied. And in sub-Christian religions the evidences of God were not found there but rather in striking and important phenomena which were first regarded vaguely as acts of divine power and later discriminated as miracles or breaks in the order of nature that evinced divine activity. Explicit belief in God on a sub-Christian level gives external support to man's moral judgments, but it confuses and diverts man's need of making explicit the faith implied in his moral activity. And at the present day much even of the thought of Christendom suffers from the same defect : its assumption that we cannot be sure of God without miracle is on the sub-Christian level.

But the miracle-accredited God is not only inadequate to man's moral needs, but, with the increasing incredibility of miracles, is losing all hold on the mind. The scientific view of the universe throws the mind of to-day back upon the implications of life for its belief in God, and upon the implications of human goodness for its belief in the divine goodness. This is an advantage, for we have seen that the grounds of belief in a good God can be found only there.

But our experience is, as we saw (pp. 123 f.), that, however surely a good God may be implied in moral activity, we fail to make this an explicit faith with equal sureness. Why is this ? It appears to result from our failure to act in accordance with it. For if faith in the dominance of a good God in the universe is to be made explicit, His goodness must dominate our own being. If it does not, then our own activity is a series of facts denying His kingship, and we have based our conscious handling of life upon an assumption incompatible with faith in His dominance. The latter point seems to be the important one, for though we failed here and there to act in harmony with the goodness of God, it could and would be truly dominant in us, provided we had a supreme desire for its dominance and were therefore making progress in that direction.

The fact seems to be that God's goodness, however surely implied in our own moral activity, is not, as there implied, of sufficiently high quality to engage our entire devotion and so to achieve actual dominance. To live in accordance with it is to live urged by a persistent monitor who demands great effort and sacrifice, but is not capable of kindling a supreme enthusiasm. Moments come when the demand is so great that its fulfilment needs a devotion more unfeigned and whole-hearted than the idea of God so implied is capable of evoking. At such times the right demands absolute devotion, but the goodness of God implied in the idea of right is not great enough to kindle absolute devotion. Hence an inward contradiction between faith and experience must come sooner or later even to the man who always strove his utmost to do the right.

But the case is complicated by the fact that we have not constantly and faithfully striven to do our best. We have done and do things that are opposed to the purpose of the universe as reflected in our idea of right. In fact, we have to recognize that the whole tenor of our life is in discord with it. The dominance of a good God is implied in our idea of right : His dominance is defied by our wrong acts and life. How is our faith in God affected by our wrong-doing ? In our best moments, when we hold to what we are sure of in God, we condemn and hate ourselves for our disloyalty. We are sure that there is in God an intense antagonism to the wrong that thwarts His good purpose, but we have in ourselves no means of getting beyond that knowledge, or rather of being sure of anything beyond it. We thus find only a divine endorsement of our self-condemnation. Between ourselves and God our wrong seems to have set a barrier which makes it impossible for us to bring our thought of God into any but a dispiriting and forbidding connection with ourselves.

Thus, so long as we are confined to the idea of God

as reflected in the ordinary moral consciousness, we find only such an idea as, when made explicit, fails to hold its own,—such an idea as, in face of the difficulty of doing right, is not high enough to evoke a triumphant and absolute loyalty. And in face of the experience of having done wrong it gives us only the paralysing assurance that God is antagonistic to wrong. And we are apt to meet this situation by turning to activities in which we can forget such thoughts. Hence our inwardly grounded faith in Him grows confused and weak, and we try to build faith on other grounds, with the result that we get an idea of God that still further confuses the issues of life, and is likely under criticism to collapse into positive unfaith.

These considerations help to explain how it is that with the entry of Jesus into our thought we become as sure of the idea of God made explicit in Him as we are of the sense of direction in our own hearts. For in Him moral activity achieves such a height that the God implied in it evokes our entire devotion. In Him we know that God loves and seeks the sinner. In Him our idea of God wins a goodness intense and pure enough to triumph over and assimilate elements that remain unconquered and unabsorbed by such a comparatively mediocre idea of God as is implied in our own moral consciousness. In Him for the first time the religious faith implied in all human moral consciousness gets, because of His moral stature, such contents that it can approve its validity over the whole range of human experience, for in Him we attain faith in a God able to command the utmost of our loyalty.

The power of Jesus to make us know God depends ultimately upon the validity of what is implied in human moral consciousness, His and ours. By our own moral consciousness we are sure that He is

and has ever since been the dominant influence in its continuance.[1]   And because He thus leads in the centre line of life's development, we cannot but think that, more than all else, He is of significance in revealing the true nature of life.

Then we find that this man, with His abysmally penetrative thought and His uncompromising hatred of pretence and sham, was convinced that He knew God. And so convinced was He that, despite all His compassion, He did not hesitate to call men to suffer for His truth's sake. We see that upon this conviction He built the most beautiful and effective life the world has known. And considering these things we find it impossible to think that God is unknowable and that all that makes Jesus significant is the greatness of His mistake. It is from any point of view more credible that such results grew from truth rather than from error.

Thus, considered as a fact of history, Jesus, by what He was, frees us from the pressure of suspicions that the ultimate reality of the world is non-moral or unknowable. For in loyalty to truth we are bound to reject any theory of the universe that does not do justice to the facts of His life, and we are sure that no mechanical or agnostic theory can do so. We are disloyal to life if we are satisfied without an answer to life's problem that is adequate to His life.

It may perhaps be said that we are not claiming enough, for the life of Jesus taken merely as a historic fact demands the theory of a good God as an explanation of the universe and gives to such an explanation as high a degree of probability as is possessed by the best established scientific theories. This may be so, especially if the life of Jesus be taken in conjunction

[1] For a further development of this line of thought see next chapter and the author's *Essays in Christian Thinking*, chap. xii.

with, and as related to, the whole development of life and personality. But it must be borne in mind that a rational probability cannot provide the basis for religious and moral faith. For when a man acts on a rational probability he is bound, in loyalty to truth, to bear in mind that it is only a probability and that he may prove mistaken in acting on it. But the affirmations that are at the base of moral activity cannot be so regarded. We cannot make mental reservations as to whether after all self-preference may not prove better than justice and more in accord with the nature of things. Our faith in justice must be absolute, and that absoluteness cannot come from any argument that only establishes probabilities.

But it may be said that some such line of argument, establishing a probable conclusion from observable premises, is the only sort of persuasion to which the scientific mind is amenable. Therein lies its usefulness. But it must be remembered that the scientific attitude is one in which the intelligence is as far as possible abstracted from the personality as a whole and especially from its active elements and from the emotional forces behind them. It can therefore give us the truth only from one specialized aspect of life and not the truth as a whole. And yet this point of view is so important to the modern mind that criticism from it must be disarmed. Some degree of arguable probability must therefore be established before our minds as a whole can rest in any affirmation. Scientific reasoning can veto an unsound element in religious and moral faith, and therefore our faith must be free from its condemnation, and this purpose is served by argument from observed facts to probable theories. A fairly high degree of arguable probability is needed, if we are to feel quite free from the criticism of our scientific mind, but it must be remembered that this is not, and cannot be, the basis of our positive faith, which needs an absolute sureness such as no argument from probability can give.

We have here a phase of what has often been remarked as characteristic of all argument about the existence of God, i.e. that it is far easier to attack antagonistic theories than to establish the positive proposition. It is easy to show that materialism can give no account of consciousness and that agnosticism contradicts itself by asserting that a man may know enough of God to know that He is unknowable. But it is not so easy to prove the existence of a personal God or to show what can be known about God. The real force in the ordinary arguments for the existence of God lies, not in what they can positively prove, but in their power to discredit the opposing positions and to disarm scientific criticism ; and in this the life of Jesus, considered as a historic fact, gives point and power. In the matter of religious faith, reason dealing with observable fact, can do little more than clear a place for the positive, absolute answer that we find within us, implied and affirmed in the highest activities of our being. Reason exposes the usurper of life's throne, but life alone can supply the occupant

(8)

When we turn to examine more closely the reaction of Jesus upon the faith implied in our moral judg ments, we can put it thus : Our inward sense of direction recognizes the fullest imaginable achieve ment of human goodness in Jesus. It recognizes its own maturity and perfection in Him. We are sure that, in so far as we do not shape life to make toward Him, we are false to ourselves. We find, therefore, i

Him an extension of the meaning and purpose of the universe as implied in our assured knowledge of right. But the main point is here, that through Jesus' interpretation of our innermost life we get a better idea of God than we can find in ourselves. And the goodness of God revealed in Him is of such a sort that it becomes effectively dominant in those that receive it. They really desire to enthrone it in their hearts, and so it overcomes progressively the wrong desires and deeds that disprove lesser thoughts of God. Faith in such a God is therefore able to remain in triumphant and saving explicitness. The moral dominance of Jesus and His power to give us a dominating and therefore explicitly credible thought of God are two aspects of one and the same thing.

When we ask what it is in Jesus that gives Him this significance, we see in the first place that He entirely lacks that self-preference which in us offends the impartiality of reason. He was loyal in act to a principle which we recognize but do not act upon. Then we see that the power behind His loyalty was a love so pure and intense as to be hardly aware of its entire self-abnegation, a love that sought at all costs the good of His fellows and knew no good apart from theirs. In Him we discover that life and intelligence are made one only in the largest and purest love, and we know that along His way lies the one way in which our self-conscious life can be true to, and at one with, itself.

And since in this aspect of Jesus' goodness we find the way which we are sure is right for us, we find also what God means and thinks concerning us and therefore all that we can know of what God is. We find thus a God of such commanding goodness and love that we cannot but love Him whole-heartedly, and

12

want Him to be enthroned effectively in our desires and deeds.

But the quality of the goodness that is characteristic of Jesus is the love that seeks the lost and speaks in the words, " But I say unto you, Love your enemies." And it is precisely this and this alone that overcomes the cleavage which our wrongdoing makes between our actual self and the God implied in our sense of right. Left to ourselves, all that we can know of God's attitude to our wrongdoing is that, since it thwarts His good purpose, He must be intensely and essentially antagonistic to it. And this thought excludes God's help where we need it most. But in Jesus, and especially in His death, we learn more of what our wrong-doing means to God. Seeing God's love in the love that Jesus had for men, we know that God loves us in spite of the sin which obstructs and defeats His good will and therefore pains His love. Our wrong-doing no longer puts us out of reach of God's help. When we thus come to know God through Jesus, we hate all that is contrary to His love and we so love Him that, despite many weaknesses and failings, we do become at heart growingly loyal to His kingship. And thus we become able to believe heartily in the dominance of His love in the universe.

This spontaneous reaction of our inward being by which Jesus is recognized as the fulfiller of our moral trend and the interpreter of God, finds justification in His own consciousness. The Man who realized the moral ideal was conscious of having a unique knowledge of God and a unique fellowship with God, which inspired and bound Him to the task of making men know God and of thus bringing them into His kingdom.

The validity of Jesus' truth of God may be summarized as follows. We are absolutely sure of a right way for us even when we do not take it. This assurance implies the assurance of a dominating purpose and good will in the universe. But we fail to convert this implication into an explicit faith because the God so implied is not good enough to evoke our whole-hearted loyalty, and our disloyalty is a fact that denies His dominance. But in Jesus we see a goodness so convincingly high and human as to imply and express a God who does take the whole homage of our hearts and does dominate our inmost being, and therefore can be explicitly believed in. And He dominates us the more the more explicitly we bring our faith in Him to bear upon the facts and acts of life. The validity of the idea of God thus made explicit is precisely the same as the validity of the assertion that there is a right way for us even when we do not take it. Contemplating Jesus, we are absolutely sure that His spirit and way are the right spirit and way for man, and this assurance involves the judgment that reality is dominated by a goodness such as His. For, since we draw all that we are from the universe, nothing but that which dominates it has right to dominate us with the absolute authority which the goodness of Jesus exercises over us.

It will confirm our thought to mark that unless God is such as we see in Jesus, He can never command the whole loyalty of man, and therefore the universe can never find its unity in Him, nor can we ever be at one with that which gave us being.

(9)

It will be well at this point to note how our conclusions affect certain objections that are commonly urged against an ethical interpretation of reality.

It is difficult to derive thought from matter, and yet human thought emerged in the universal process of evolution. This induces many thinkers to allow that the fundamental reality must have some elements analogous to our mental powers. But if so much must be granted to bring the fact of human thought into intelligible relation with our idea of the whole, why not go on and add to our idea of the fundamental reality what is necessary to make man's moral consciousness an intelligible part of the whole ? And there has yet to be suggested any theory of existence that is able to do this except that which involves belief in a good God. But against this belief certain objections have been urged.

If a man's idea of the fundamental reality of the universe is not a genuine faith but a make-believe, he will be living upon a self-deception. Hence he must be very careful not to let his judgment be prejudiced by his desires. And he may easily suspect that to believe in a good God is to succumb to this temptation. He may doubt whether religion is not man's overweening self-regard projecting itself into the universe. This objection might apply to belief in a God whose goodness was of a mediocre sort. But the goodness of God revealed by Jesus is of such sort that it humbles man, demands from him a complete surrender of all private claims, and so is free from the suspicion of being the projection of man's self-conceit and self-concern.

A more serious difficulty brought against belief in a good God is the pain and moral evil in the world. How can these things exist in a world made or dominated by a good Will ?

With regard to pain, the usual reply is that pain seems to be an unavoidable concomitant of life and sensibility, that in animal life there is a considerable overplus of pleasure, that in man much of the pain suffered is merited and that if there were no possibility of unmerited suffering there could be no heroism or self-sacrifice.

But the problem of pain cannot be adequately treated apart from that of moral evil, for the two problems meet in the problem of moral freedom. To deny the moral freedom of man is to say that man is not responsible for his acts and so practically to deny the existence of moral evil in the world. But to do so is to aggravate the problem of pain. For if moral freedom is denied, moral values lose their base, and pain and pleasure become the final counters of life. And to remove the validity of moral values is to make the higher pleasures deceptive and to leave unquestioned only those that are sensuous ; it is also to destroy that dignity of initiative which mitigates and transforms suffering. Consequently the denial of human freedom involves a view of life in which pleasure and pain are the only criterions of value and in which pain generally predominates. And it is, of course, impossible to think of a good God as the ultimate reality of such a universe. Of all this we have a striking picture in Hardy's *Dynasts*, where, against a background that denies all human initiative, heroism appears a pathetic futility and life an " intolerable antilogy."

But if we admit the moral freedom of man, it allows the usual answer to the problem of moral evil, i.e. that a real moral goodness in man cannot exist without moral freedom, that moral freedom involves the possibility of choosing the wrong, that God, being good, must desire that man should be capable of possessing moral goodness and must therefore allow man the possibility of choosing wrongly, i.e. must allow the possibility of moral evil.

This answer has difficulties of its own. It seems to compromise the sovereignty of God in order to save His goodness. But we can hardly be sure that it does save His goodness until we have answered the question, What does it mean to God when man chooses the wrong ? For it does not seem right that a Creator should expose His creatures to a risk which He does not in some way share, however much they may be to blame for their fate. And it becomes clear that these difficulties can be overcome only if we can believe God's goodness to be like the goodness of Jesus. For if we see the love of God in the love that Jesus had for man, then we know that man's wrong-doing is pain to God, i.e. that God does not leave man alone to bear the risk created by the divine allowance of the possibility of evil. In Jesus God reveals the full height and depth of His love to man by suffering for his sake and thus claims our devotion with the only authority to which man can whole-heartedly give himself. And so God, in compromising His sovereignty by giving man freedom, does it to so Godlike a length that He gains the only possible means to sovereignty over the human heart.

And if God is willing to bear pain for the sake of good and can attain the highest good for His world in no other way, we have a consideration which reflects on the problem of pain. Especially it suggests that in unmerited human pain there is, or may be, a peculiar fellowship with God and a peculiar knowledge of His divinest power,—" Blessed are they that have been persecuted for righteousness' sake : for theirs is the kingdom of heaven " or " the kingship of God " (Matt. v. 10).

(10)

The view of the gospel here set forth may be thought to share the difficulty of all faiths that centre round a historic person. It may be objected that it depends ultimately upon the historicity of the Gospel narrative and is therefore at the mercy of historic criticism, and that in any case no record of long-past events can give us the sureness that is required as a base for religious faith.

But it has been shown that the sureness of our faith does not depend upon our sureness of any historic fact but upon our sureness of a direction in life, of a way that we ought to go, whether we do go by it or not. Jesus reacts upon this sureness, not as an external authority, but as One in whom this internal authority comes to a full knowledge of itself and so gets power to become definite and dominant. "But," it may be persisted, "you depend upon the Gospel narrative for your knowledge of the One who so reacts upon your moral consciousness, and if the record is not reliable, must not the reaction be repudiated?"

It seems, however, that only one conceivable criticism could destroy the gospel as here defined. If it could be proved that the goodness of the Man portrayed in the first three Gospels was impossible, that such a character could not possibly have been, then we should have no gospel. But it is not within the scope of any legitimate criticism to pronounce such a verdict, which could proceed only from an assumption as to the nature of the universe and not from the application of any canon of historic or literary criticism.

But to grant that such a goodness is possible is to affirm reality to be of such a nature as to make it possible. That is, the existence of the picture of the Jesus of the first three Gospels is itself a gospel, if we grant that it is the picture of a not impossible goodness. Such a goodness is possible only in the same sort of universe as would be evinced by its actual existence. For it is our conception of the nature of the universe that governs our conclusions as to what is possible or impossible.

It is necessary to be clear on this point. It may be said that it is easy enough to imagine a man performing wonders which could not be proved to be impossible and which, if believed, would radically alter our idea of the universe ; and yet we should not, because we could not prove such wonders impossible, allow them a determinative place in our thoughts. But it is different when we are speaking of moral qualities. For when a moral quality is portrayed and we pronounce it impossible, we at the same time really deny that it is good, for there is no moral obligation to attempt the impossible. Of course, we may imagine a goodness impossible here and now to every man, but it is a contradiction in terms to speak of an imagined human goodness as humanly impossible. So that to allow that a certain act or character is good is to assert that it is possible, and to assert that it is possible is to say something about human nature and about the universe that produced human nature.

Therefore to put before human eyes the picture of a man whom the beholder recognizes to be better than any he has yet seen is epoch-making to the beholder. Just in so far as the goodness depicted is convincingly, positively good, and not merely a negative, lifeless absence of evil, it will react upon his moral consciousness and upon the therein implied judgment as to the nature of reality. And the first three Gospels stand absolutely alone in the depicting of a positively and completely good man.

It is fantastic to attempt to regard the character of Jesus in the synoptic record as a work of creative fiction, for there is too much evidence of a multiplicity of sources and traditions and differences of standpoint. But if we could so regard it, there would be considerable reason for thinking that its author possessed the character he depicted. For the world lacks another case of a writer being able to depict a convincingly vital character better than any known at the time. The greatest artists in characterization do not attempt to depict perfect character. And even when, with Jesus before him, the writer of fiction or poetry attempts an ideal man, he is always, like Tennyson's Arthur, inclined to be bloodless and negative, and is always less human than Jesus. A poet, of course, may see and revere and depict a man better than himself, but there is no instance of poetry or fiction bringing into the world a hitherto unknown level and standard of goodness. Imagination may create an ideal beauty greater than any yet seen in the world, but it would seem that in morals the creative artist must be the good man himself. Nor is this really an exception, for after all the man who imagines better beauty than he sees does but give to the world the embodiment of his own inward beauty. A Jew, able to invent a convincingly real and positive human character who taught his fellow Jews to love their enemies, could hardly have done so without having first lived through the experience he depicted. The world's new advances in character and goodness have never been won by fiction, but by flesh and blood and living spirit.

And we should come to the same conclusion if we accepted the still more fantastic suggestion that the character of Jesus is the work of legendary accretion. Here we should have to suppose an indefinite company of creative spiritual geniuses all as great and good as the man to whose picture they contributed. But the whole experience of history is rather that legend debases the goodness of its hero, dehumanizes him and makes his wonders trivial, and never creates an advance in the moral standard.

It will have been remarked that these considerations take us far beyond the point at which they started. Once we grant that the character of Jesus is possible, that is, that He is good (and this is all that is absolutely necessary for our gospel), we are compelled to go on to acknowledge that simple loyalty to overwhelming probability compels us to conclude that a real Man stood for the portrait given us in the first three Gospels. There are, no doubt, legendary elements even in them. Sometimes the process is seen at work in the modifications which the later evangelists, the first and third, introduced into what they took over from Mark and which generally give an enhanced picture of the miraculous powers of Jesus, but never add to our idea of His goodness. The same may be said of the Fourth Gospel and, with much greater emphasis, of the apocryphal Gospels. So that critical considerations go to support the conclusion arrived at on general grounds that the character of Jesus as given in the Synoptic Gospels is not capable of other explanation than that Jesus was so.

It will be thus seen that a gospel that is concerned above all with the character of Jesus will not only do ample justice to the inestimable value of the Gospel record, but will welcome eagerly all critical processes that can enable us to distinguish between what is due to the development of tradition or to the evangelist's own mind and what are the simple memoirs of Jesus' life and teaching. And those who are acquainted with the more generally accepted results of New Testament criticism will know that the effect of distinguishing the less authentic parts of the record is to enhance the inner unity and the moral and spiritual supremacy of Jesus. Criticism cleans the picture and adds appreciably to the distinctness and convincing beauty of the face in which we see " the light of the knowledge of the glory of God."

CHAPTER VI

THEOLOGICAL

(1)

THE traditional gospel can be effectively preached only to those who have already accepted certain theological propositions. They must believe certain things about God and His ways with men and about the person of Jesus. And year by year the people of whom this can be assumed grow fewer.

On the other hand, the proclamation that, because of what Jesus was in character and word and deed, His thought of God may be ours, is a gospel that depends upon no theological presuppositions. It does not even demand faith in God : it creates it. It is therefore essentially the gospel for to-day.

And the difference between these two situations effects the whole body and method of our religious thinking. If in Jesus alone we get the experience of an assured and effective belief in God, then that experience must be regulative of the whole of our theology. We shall find partial and tentative revelations elsewhere,—all helpful, but all subject for their value and validity to the indubitable assurance of God that we have through the reaction of Jesus upon our moral consciousness. We are compelled to confess that " No man . . . knoweth the Father, save the Son, and he to whomsoever the Son willeth to reveal Him " (Matt. xi. 27, Luke x. 22).

This consideration reflects first upon the nature of religious faith. The faith in God that Jesus gives us lies in the union of two pronouncements which we cannot doubt even if we try to, i.e. that there is a right direction for us in life whether we take it or not, and that in Jesus we see the spirit and way that is right for us. Of the one thing in life of which we are sure Jesus gives us an interpretation that cannot be doubted so long as the mind contemplates the fact of His goodness. And religious belief does not help us unless it is of this sort, i.e. belief in what we cannot disbelieve. Beliefs that need to be supported are a burden. Nor is our honesty helped by any belief to which we are not compelled in loyalty to truth.

This free and inward conviction is quite different from the assurance that comes by suggestion. It is particularly necessary to note this, because the religious value of belief induced by suggestion has been overestimated and its dangers overlooked. If the full truth of God is found only in Christ, then we ought to be quite sure of God only through Him. An imperfect idea of God's goodness involves an inconsistent idea of God, and to be sure of an inconsistent idea indicates the work of suggestion, not of free conviction, and involves both mental and moral danger.

In some quarters people are still asked to take their beliefs upon the authority of the Church. This is defended on the plea that we take many of our practical beliefs on authority. But here three things may be said :—

(a) In practical life, belief on authority is considered justifiable only where the matter is of relative unimportance or where the real grounds of belief are inaccessible to the ordinary individual.

(b) Belief on authority can never give absolute assurance. In religion it is always only too possible to doubt what is given on authority and to question the validity of the authority itself ; for there are different authorities that differ between themselves in their statements as to what is to be believed. And this casts a doubt even upon those things in which they agree.

(c) Authority cannot therefore be the right channel for the most assured sort of belief. And even those who recommend belief on authority assume that an inward conviction is possible and is in part, at least, the source of the Church's authority. But if it is assumed that grounds of inward belief are available to men and that it is desirable that they should ultimately come to such an inwardly grounded belief, then it follows that to encourage belief on authority is to hinder their arrival at the desired state. For a true belief is belief in things that we cannot disbelieve, and in order to discover these the critical faculty is necessary, while to accept a belief on authority is to renounce criticism. It has been a very common experience that beliefs taken on authority must be shattered before we can advance to a living faith.

Another common method of dealing with the doubter is to tell him to suppress his questionings and to live and act as though he believed and that he will in course of time find that his doubts have vanished. But even if we are sure that we have infallible truth, are we right in asking a man to acquire belief in it by any other means than by being convinced that it is true ? This method is sometimes defended on the ground that it is similar to the way in which a scientific hypothesis becomes confirmed by being employed as a working theory. But the comparison will not hold. In science, when a working theory is presented to us, we are not asked to allow it to affect our judgments and experience in order

that we may cease to have any doubts about it.
Rather, in using a working theory, it is scientifically
essential to keep an open mind as to its truth and to
be on the watch for any experience that may contradict or modify it. To act on a scientific theory is
not to cease to question it, but to be continually
questioning it in the most searching way.

The effect of this method of dealing with religious
doubt,—and it is undoubtedly effective,—depends upon
the fact that it deals with material largely different
from the material of science. In science, if you act
upon an unsound theory, your very act will be likely
to make its unsoundness apparent. But in many
moral and religious concerns, to act on a belief, whether
it is true or false, helps to confirm it. Beliefs of
this sort, when we act on them, grow more real to
us, and, when we do not act on them, they become
shadowy and unreal. Thus a belief in lucky numbers
or lucky days, in charms or superstitions, is likely
to grow as we act upon it. The same is true of suspicion of an individual and of general cynicism : the
more you act on them, the more you will believe in
them. A psychological process is at work here that
is equally effective in confirming either true or false
belief. It is clear, therefore, that this method of
dealing with doubt cannot put a man in right relationship to the truth. The only honest method in
religion is to act because we are convinced, not in
order that we may be convinced. Otherwise we
are only adding auto-suggestion to the suggestion of
authority and putting an additional wall of habit
between ourselves and a true inward belief.

To suppress questioning when once it has arisen is
to make the mind incapable of being inwardly convinced of the truth. For when the mind is presented
with a proposition that rouses a doubt, the solution

of that doubt is obviously a necessary condition to the honest acceptance of the proposition. To secure its acceptance in any other way is to secure its acceptance for some other reason than because it is true. This dishonours truth and at the same time permanently dulls the mind's sensitiveness to it. When questioning is suppressed, a tame credence is obtained by the excision of those most vital elements of thought that are man's only security against complete dominance by suggestion.

In such methods of cultivating belief the questionings of the mind are not answered and are treated as though they were incapable of answer and inimical to life. This is only a variant of the old method of protecting the truth of the Church of Christ by taking the life of all questioners. It tends to a permanent divorce between a man's religion and the spontaneity of his thought. The shirked struggle for truth grows harder and harder to resume, and the ecclesiastical opiate becomes a necessity of life.

Thus, however we approach the matter, we come to the same conclusion, that if it is in Jesus only that we know God fully and surely by inward conviction, then the sooner we leave other methods and accept the gospel He preached, the better will it be for our honesty and faith.

(2)

The experience created by the gospel must be the field and norm of Christian theology. In the New Testament writers we see that the main driving and directing power of their thought was their experience of the power of the gospel of Jesus. And it may be argued, " Why not then be content with the theology of the New Testament ? " To which it must be replied that there is in the New Testament no easily and surely observable system of thought that can be called a theology, otherwise such diverse theologies would not claim New Testament authority. We have noted also (pp. 54 ff.) that in New Testament thinking there are several elements of Jewish thought, not only foreign, but even contradictory, to the thought of Jesus. This is what might be expected, since the thought of Jesus was in so many respects revolutionary, while the writers of the New Testament were mostly, if not all, men who had been born in, and had already absorbed, the Judaic or the Hellenistic tradition before their acceptance of Jesus as Lord. We have also to allow for the fact that their thought, as we have it, was mostly shaped to meet the needs of men with other ways of mind than ours.

From this point of view we must consider their idea of the law and of scripture generally. The Christian faith involves the contention that the revelation of God in Jesus is true because it gives us the only conception of God and life that is not self-contradictory. From which it follows that any idea of God lower than that which we have from Jesus contains elements of self-contradiction that diminish its credibility. And to be perfectly sure of what is inconsistent is to be handicapped in the reception of further light. It may perhaps be said that this is not borne out in the case of the teachers of Israel, who were very sure of God on a level lower than that of the teaching of Jesus and who nevertheless led up to Him. But what we are now discussing is a sureness of God as made explicit for conscious thought, whereas the central sureness of Israel's teachers was in the " Thus saith the Lord " of the moral command, which is really not so much an explication of the God implied in moral judgments as the asseveration that He is implied in it. It gives in religious language the absoluteness of the moral obligation. When they went beyond this and made their thought of God explicit, they were not always right. We have, for instance, the whole Mosaic legislation given as with direct divine authority, and yet we find Jeremiah (vii. 22, 23) denying the divine origin of the ritual section of the law. Jeremiah's great prophecy of the new covenant recognized that Israel was not yet properly sure of God. And it was along the line of his thought that Hebrew religion reached its highest. So that side by side with the prophetic sureness of God, which is characteristically evident in the moral command, there was prophetic recognition of something lacking in sureness of an explicit, comprehensive thought of God.

From the Christian conviction that only in Jesus do we get a self-consistent thought of God we may therefore argue that to be perfectly sure of God as a moral being, but as one of less goodness than the God of Jesus, is to have a serious obstacle to the right understanding and acceptance of His truth. Now the Jews of Jesus' day were quite sure of God, an assurance grounded especially in their idea of the directly divine origin of the law. And the God of whom they were sure was not a God with the moral quality of goodness that Jesus knew in God. The result of this was that most of them were in bitter opposition to Jesus, and even those who accepted Him as Messiah were hindered in their understanding of Him. The Jew with this sort of belief as to God's relationship to the law and to the scriptures generally demanded that the truth of Jesus should accredit itself to his prior belief in one or both of two ways :—

(a) It must be shown to be perfectly consistent with the already accepted revelation. Hence the attempt must be made to proceed logically from the

older to the newer revelation, i.e. from the less consistent to the more consistent, which is impossible ;
and the attempt is bound to result in a dilution of
the new by the old.

(b) It must prove its divine authority by the
acknowledged methods of the scriptures, the voice
from heaven, fire from heaven, or some other
indubitable " sign."

We have seen (pp. 54 and 60) that both these
premises are foreign to the thought of Jesus. When
Jesus said that He came to fulfil the law (Matt. v. 17),
and did so by overriding it in more than one particular (Matt. v. 38, 39, 43, 44 ; Mark vii. 14, 15,
x. 5–9 ; John v. 16, 17), He implied that the law was
imperfect and inconsistent in itself. In the Mosaic
law of divorce He saw a departure from the divine
order and a concession to human evil (Mark x. 5).
With regard to His repudiation of " signs " we may
add to the evidence already considered (p. 61) a
saying which a number of important manuscripts
add to Luke ix. 55, " Ye know not what manner of
spirit ye are of." This was His answer to James
and John, who supported their suggestion for fire
from heaven by a reference to Elijah, and it is a
repudiation either of the historicity or of the heavenly
origin of Elijah's fire,—which is sufficient to account
for the omission of it from other manuscripts.

To us it is the goodness of Jesus that first makes us
really sure of God. The Jew was already sure of
God and demanded assurance that what he saw in
Jesus was true of God. Especially did he feel this
with regard to the death of Jesus. The Mosaic connection of prosperity with godliness made it very
difficult for the Jew to accept a crucified Messiah.
We have seen (pp. 55 ff.) how this difficulty reacted
on the early Church's understanding of the death

of Jesus and created a tendency to interpret it
in the terms of sin-offering and how, supported by
the Jewish craving for signs, it also emphasized
the importance of the resurrection as a miraculous
endorsement of Jesus' Messiahship. The former point
has already been fully considered, and it is the latter
that chiefly concerns us now.

The attitude of mind that regarded the resurrection as the supreme attesting miracle, as God's
especial seal to the validity of Jesus' Messiahship,
was a retrogression from the spiritual purity of the
first confession at Cæsarea Philippi. For there, in
contrast with the multitude who saw only the works
of healing and thought Jesus a prophet, the Twelve,
with their more intimate fellowship, confessed, " Thou
art the Christ " (Mark viii. 29), and, so confessing,
evoked the response of Jesus, " Flesh and blood hath
not revealed it, but My Father which is in heaven"
(Matt. xvi. 17). To regard the resurrection as an
attesting sign was to disregard Jesus' teaching that
moral and spiritual truth must be its own evidence
and that if that does not suffice, "neither will they
be persuaded, if one rise from the dead " (Luke xvi.
31). And if it is answered that the miracle of the
resurrection did win belief, then this saying of Jesus
suggests, what we shall see to be true, that the belief
so induced carried into Christianity elements that
were foreign to the teaching of Jesus. Nor need we
be surprised at this when we recall the many points
at which, we are told, the disciples misunderstood
Jesus (Mark iv. 13, vii. 18, viii. 32, ix. 10, 32, 39 ;
x. 13, 24, 38, etc.).

We also find the influence of old Hebrew ideas in
the story of the ascension. The Jews were sure
from the scriptures that God lived in the heavens
above Palestine. Therefore the ascension of Jesus

was needed to complete the authentication of His miraculous resurrection.

This strong tendency to insist upon the resurrection and ascension as " signs " had further results. One of the most marked ways in which the Fourth Gospel differs from the first three (and thereby shows itself at a further remove from authenticity) is that Jesus' works of healing are said to be regarded by Him as evidential signs done to answer the Jewish demand (John iv. 48, vi. 26, xi. 15, 42). And development in this direction, once begun, was likely to go farther. For if the divine in man needs accrediting by super- natural miracle, it must be because the divine is something foreign to man. And so the logical counter- part of miraculous resurrection and ascension must be found in descent from heaven or miraculous birth. This tendency shows itself very markedly in some of the New Testament accounts of the person of Christ : in others its presence is doubtful or more than doubtful. For there is considerable variety of state- ment :—

(a) In Matt. i. we have the story of the beginning of Jesus in the miraculous conception of the Virgin Mary by the Holy Spirit, but we have to note that this account proffers itself (Matt. i. 22, 23) as the ful- filment of a prophecy which the evangelist mis- translates at the vital point by giving as " virgin " a Hebrew word that merely signified any young woman of marriageable age. It is generally claimed that Luke, in chapters i. and ii., adopts the tradition of the virgin-birth, but he does not make it explicit, and in view of what follows it is difficult to think that he believed in it. For almost immediately he speaks of Joseph and Mary as Jesus' " father and mother " (ii. 33) and as " His parents " (ii. 41) and makes Mary speak of Joseph as " Thy father "

(ii. 48). We note also that in the Fourth Gospel Philip calls Jesus " the son of Joseph " (i. 45), and that to the Jews, who know Him by the same designation (vi. 42), Jesus acknowledges, " Ye both know Me, and know whence I am " (vii. 27, 28), from which it seems that the author of the Fourth Gospel took Joseph to be the father of Jesus. And Paul, in the careful and explicit statement as to the person of Jesus with which the Epistle to the Romans opens, says nothing of His origin save that He was " born of the seed of David according to the flesh." It should be noted that the Matthæan account, which tells us that the beginning of Jesus as a personal being was when Mary conceived by the Holy Spirit, does therefore by implication deny that He was personally pre-existent.

(b) In the prologue (and only in the prologue) of the Fourth Gospel we have the Logos doctrine applied to Jesus in what seems to be a statement of the Church's belief as to the person of Jesus in the terms of current philosophy, which is apparently also found in Heb. i. 1–3 and Col. i. 15–17.

(c) In the body of the Fourth Gospel Jesus is identified with the " Son of man " who " descended out of heaven " (iii. 13, vi. 62). He is said to have spoken of Himself as having " come down from heaven " (vi. 33, 38, 50, 62) and as having been " before Abraham " (viii. 58). Here we seem to have the pre-existent, heavenly Son of man of the Similitudes of Enoch (xlviii. 2, 3 ; lxii. 7, etc.). Some scholars maintain that Paul brought with him into his Christianity a similar idea of a pre-existent heavenly Messiah analogous to the Enochian " Son of man." But against this we do not find Paul speaking in the Johannine manner of the beginning of Jesus' earthly life as " a coming down from heaven." And if we take Colossians to be Paul's, we have there an idea that approximates rather to the Logos doctrine of the prologue of the Fourth Gospel than to that of the pre-existent Messiah or Son of man.

But in both (b) and (c) the question arises as to the extent to which passages which seem to imply the pre-existence of Jesus should be understood literally. For in the New Testament we find language in which a continuity or identity of personality is verbally affirmed but is obviously not intended to be understood. Some of the Jews said that Jesus was Elijah ; others, together with Herod, said He was the Baptist (Mark vi. 13, 14 ; viii. 27, 28) : Jesus said that John was Elijah (Mark ix. 13, Matt. xvii, 12, 13). And we have to reckon also with the Jewish idea of things and persons as being pre-existent in the thought of God. Very possibly, therefore, the passages, under (b) and (c) are strained beyond the intent of their writers when they are interpreted as stating the personal pre-existence of Jesus. And there are indications that this is so. The very term " The Word " suggests rather a principle than a person, and its philosophical antecedents confirm the suggestion. The declaration, " Before Abraham was, I *am*," given in justification of the words, " Abraham rejoiced to see My day, and he saw it and was glad " (John viii. 56, 58), implies pre-existence in the intent and promise of God rather than in any other way. So too Heb. i. 1–2 must be understood in the light of i. 4, which speaks of Jesus as " having become by so much better than the angels, as He hath inherited a more excellent name than they." Had the writer thought of Jesus as personally pre-existing as the Son of God, he could hardly have spoken of Him as " becoming " better than the angels or as

" inheriting " what was already His. And if Col. i. 15–17 is to be accepted as from the pen of Paul, it must be understood in the light of such a passage as Rom. i. 1 ff., which is a formal and careful statement about the person of Jesus, but which can hardly be defended from the charge of being misleading if it was written by one who believed that Jesus preexisted. It is often argued that in Phil. ii. 5 ff. we have the idea of a pre-existent divine being who " emptied Himself " and so became the man Jesus, but it is doubtful whether this meaning is intended. The passage may, without straining, be read to apply generally to Jesus' self-humiliation in such acts as the washing of the disciples' feet. And such an interpretation is more in accord with Paul's general thought. He does not think of Jesus even in His humiliation and suffering as being the divine emptied of itself,— " in the face of Jesus Christ " is " the knowledge of the glory of God " (2 Cor. iv. 6), " Christ crucified " is " the power of God and the wisdom of God " (1 Cor. i. 23, 25).

We have to conclude that although the New Testament writers sometimes use language which implies the pre-existence of Jesus, they also use language which suggests that they did not think of Him as *personally* pre-existing. This leaves us to infer that, if their thought was consistent, they thought of Jesus as pre-existing in the mind and purpose of God or in some way other than personal pre-existence. But we are not entitled to suppose that their thinking was rigidly systematic.

The later Church, therefore, had some pretext for maintaining that the personal pre-existence of Christ was taught by the New Testament writers. In so far as this contention is justified, it illustrates what happens when those who are sure of God apart from

Jesus seek to add His truth to what they already hold. Both the Jew, with his inherited ideas about the scriptures, and the philosopher, with his idea of a self-sufficient God, had here the same interest. Neither found in his old idea of God a place for the suffering love that is so indubitably divine in Jesus. Both were tempted to make room for it by placing a second divine being alongside the deity already believed in and by holding that this second divine being was incarnated in Jesus.

The trouble is that when this is done we have no longer the same Jesus. For what is thus proffered to us as the final secret of His being proves on examination to imply that He was either God masquerading as man or God ignorantly thinking Himself man ; whereas the record shows us a man in human relation to God, a man to whom temptation was a reality and to whom, therefore, sin was a possibility, a man who prayed to God as man prays, a man who knew the possibility of a difference between God's will and His own (Mark xiv. 36). The process of thought which begins with the resurrection regarded as a miraculous sign and ends in the idea of the personal pre-existence of Jesus starts from premises which He explicitly rejected and leads to conclusions which undermine the reality of His human goodness.

We shall, however, do great injustice to the New Testament thinkers unless we remember that on the whole they did not allow their Christology to dehumanize Jesus,—a process which later became disastrously effective. It was their strong sense of His manhood that kept their Christology so tentative and variant and that withheld them from a thorough systematization of their thought. For we have here to reckon with a factor that affected all pre-evolutionary thinking.

In Hebrew thought, as expressed in the story of creation and elsewhere, the relationship of God to the world had two distinct phases, the creative and the proprietary or governmental. In creation He is present in brief, supremely divine activity, resulting in new, marvellous and lasting effects. Then He " rests," leaving the effects of His creative outgoing to persist in rhythmic but unachieving change. It was no heresy for a Jew to declare that " there is no new thing under the sun " (Eccles. i. 9). What went on in the course of nature and history was thought to be quite a different sort of activity from God's creative activity, and God was thought to be related to it in quite a different way. It proceeded on a plane that was at a considerable remove from the specifically divine activity of creation and therefore could not be expected to produce anything vitally new and divinely good. During this proprietary period anything authentically divine and blessedly new must be regarded as a momentary reversion of God to the creative phase, as a divine inbreaking on the established order.

Now in Jesus men found a divinely creative power, the coming of something blessedly new, an authentic activity of God. They could not do justice to this experience nor think intelligibly of it by regarding Jesus as belonging to that level of being in which God was only proprietary and not creative. Since they had the idea that there were two different phases of God's relation to the world, one of greater and one of less activity and intimacy, they could not but think of Jesus as belonging to the creative phase in which God was most actively and intimately present. Hence the ideas of the miraculous origin and pre-existence of Jesus. But the trouble is that a thorough prosecution of this thought removes Jesus from the specific conditions of human history and makes Him something other than man, and so confuses and obstructs our thought of Him. The New Testament writers seem to have felt this, and therefore called their thought to a halt. With the accepted idea of the two different phases of God's activity in the world, they could not systematize their thought without sacrificing either the manhood of Jesus or His religious significance, and their experience was robust enough to leave the intellectual solution in abeyance. They stated their experience in the only terms available, and the vital unity of their experience does not seem to have been much troubled because the terms available did not allow them a thorough consistency of statement. But it is hardly open to question that the Church, in its later attempts to give the religious significance of Jesus definite expression in the terms of then current thought, came to think of Him as other than man.

(3)

In considering the Jewish assurance of a knowledge of God apart from Jesus and its effect on the thought of the early Church, we are reminded that a similar state of things has persisted in Christian thought up to the present day. Men who hold to the literal inspiration and inerrancy of the Bible are in much the same position as the Jews of Jesus' time. They are quite sure that they have a veritable knowledge of God in the Old Testament apart from Jesus. The real business of their Christology is to prove that in Jesus there was a genuine and final addition to the earlier revelation. As a result, Christendom in its Christology has taken up many of those elements in the New Testament which are least in accord with

the spirit of Jesus and has supported His authority
by the appeal to miracle which He repudiated.

If we are sure of God apart from Jesus, then the
religious value of His teaching and life will depend
on our ability to establish an indubitable connection
between Him and our already accepted idea of God.
In this case the addition that Jesus makes to our
thought of God lies in an ethical and spiritual height
that it does not have without Him.   But if this is
what He adds, then we cannot prove Him divine by
appealing to His moral and spiritual height.   For
that would mean that we already knew that God
was as Jesus was in this respect.   And if we know
that already, what need for Jesus to tell us ?   Nor
can we ground the connection on something imperfect
in the moral and spiritual elements of our prior conception of God.   For how could we be confidently
sure of an idea of God that is now by newer knowledge
proved to belie His goodness ?   Clearly then, if we
are of those who come to the truth of Jesus already
persuaded that we have sure knowledge of God,
we cannot assure ourselves of the truth of Jesus by
appeal to the divine goodness but must appeal to
divine power.   Hence the importance of miracles
to this class of thought and the need to construe
the person of Jesus in miraculous, superhuman
terms.

The position with regard to " natural " religion
was similar.   It was supposed that reason could give
us a perfectly reliable though not complete knowledge of God, the additional content needing to be
supplied by revelation.   But " natural theology "
gave us mainly and essentially a God of power.   What
was looked for from revelation was assurance as to
the higher things in the character of God.   We have
therefore a repetition of the situation that God's

goodness must be authenticated by His power, the spiritual by the physical.

Thus the whole of the Roman theology and most of the Protestant came to be founded on the claim of the Church to possess truth in the shape of revelation itself miraculous or guaranteed by miracle.

This attitude shows itself characteristically in insisting that Jesus is essentially more than human in a sense that God does not mean or want other men to be. The orthodox doctrine of the person of Jesus is thus in as close and disastrous relation to the doctrine of the inerrancy of scripture as the orthodox doctrine of His death is to the doctrine of eternal torment.

This position involves the assumption that unless men could believe in the virgin-birth of Jesus, His pre-existence, His miraculous resurrection and His ascension, they would not know why they should obey Him and accept the authority of His ethical and religious teaching. And yet if any man were to ask himself whether Jesus would have us obey Him and accept His truth for such reasons or because our inward sense of right responds to His teaching and life as to no other, there can be no doubt as to the answer.

The popular version of orthodox Christology is based on the idea that God dwells out of the world and above it, from whence He occasionally modifies mundane processes. Hence Jesus to be authentically divine must " come down from heaven " and must return by ascending through the sky into heaven. God is thought to be in Himself essentially apart from the world. Hence no man born into the world could possibly be really the Son of God or be wholly loyal to God unless he had previously lived as God with God in heaven. This represents not unfairly

the ideas of the large mass of Christian people who
to-day consider themselves orthodox, who find no
difficulty in accepting the whole of their respective
historic creeds and confessions, and who form the
support of the reputedly orthodox thinkers of their
several Churches. These thinkers themselves would
probably repudiate some of the cruder of such
notions, which have nevertheless been allowed to
persist.

The result of this theology has been largely to
stultify the revelation of Jesus. The popular God of
Christendom has been the God of the Old Testament
and not often even of the Old Testament at its highest
level. He was nominally a just God but one who
punished sin with a cruelty that would have enhanced
the reputation of Nero. His love was confined to
comparatively few and the cost of it fell on someone
else. In common life He was mainly known as the
power that controlled accident and disaster and
death and such physical and other conditions as
make for good crops and weather and health and
business prosperity. Neither in Christian theology
nor in popular Christianity has Jesus' thought of
God been effectively dominant. It has been allowed
to make only a fugitive, occasional and uncertain
addition to an idea of God which is otherwise mainly
below the level of His thought.

The very nature of the revelation of God in Jesus
is such that it must repudiate all attempt to authenti-
cate it by miracle. His revelation is that God is
love, that goodness is supreme in the ultimate reality.
Now we cannot believe goodness to be supreme in
the universe unless we give it supremacy in ourselves.
And we can give goodness a true supremacy in ourselves only by making it supreme for its intrinsic
value. The enthroning of goodness for its own sake

does undoubtedly imply the belief that in God power is subservient to goodness. But if we wait to be assured that power will back goodness before we enthrone goodness, we are enthroning not goodness but power. Therefore any attempt to give goodness a premier place by the countersignature of power is self-contradictory, for it makes goodness secondary to power. If you lend for friendship's sake, you do not ask for securities : if you trust a man's truth, you do not also ask for evidence : you even repudiate it, if offered. Hence all miracle of event or of person adduced to support the revelation of God in Jesus can do nothing but defeat its own end.

Many modern theologians, though they have relinquished the idea of biblical inerrancy and no longer rely upon miracle as the ultimate authentication, and though they maintain that the conclusive evidence of Jesus' divinity lies in His moral and spiritual supremacy, yet assert that they find themselves still obliged to hold to the miraculous in His person and circumstance. They regard the virgin-birth or pre-existence of Jesus, His miraculous resurrection and ascension, not as authenticating His truth, but as necessary concomitants of what He was. They do not seem to see how revolutionary is their change of position with regard to biblical inerrancy and authenticating miracle. If a man says that he cannot accept Jesus' truth of God unless he can know Him pre-existent and virgin-born, the position is un-Christian but intelligible. If we say that to us Jesus is morally and spiritually supreme by right of what He was in character and spirit apart from all question of origin, we are undoubtedly accepting His supremacy as He would have it accepted ; but how then can we plead that pre-existence and virgin-birth are necessities of thought ? They can be necessary only if they are necessary to explain the moral and spiritual supremacy of Jesus. But can you explain the goodness of a man? Or if you can, does it not always diminish the goodness just in so far as you are successful in explaining it?

One thing only is made a necessity of thought by all that Jesus was and by the power He has in the experience of men, and that is, that His thought of God was true. All other presuppositions react harmfully. If, for instance, we say that such goodness as we see in Him is impossible in a merely human being, therefore we must conclude that He had a uniquely divine origin, then we quite clearly imply that such goodness would have been more wonderful had it been purely human. We therefore lessen its wonder and moral power by stipulating for the superhuman. The more we insist on finding the secret of Jesus in anything other than sheer moral and spiritual supremacy, the more we obscure and diminish both the content and credibility of His truth.

And a more direct reaction upon our thought of God is involved. For if a virgin-birth was possible and necessary and capable of producing a perfect man, why did not God make all births virgin-births? And if to be sinless implies other than common human origin, how are men of ordinary birth to blame for their sinfulness? To account for Jesus by miracle is to say that He is different from other men because in His case God did something that He is not willing to do in the case of other men. But if the goodness of Jesus has a presupposition that ours must lack, He cannot be our moral ideal. If God is not willing to do for all men what He did for Jesus, He cannot want all men to be like Him, and Jesus is therefore not the interpreter of God's will nor the revealer of God's character.

(4)

For the greater part of the thinking and educated people of to-day miracle has lost its evidential value. Even for those who find a break in the order of nature conceivable, such an event needs more evidence than it affords. And this is an advantage, because it throws us back upon the moral and spiritual supremacy of Jesus for our conviction of His right to speak for God. It relieves us of the temptation to "seek after a sign," and so removes an ancient hindrance to the understanding of Jesus' truth. To this extent it gives us an advantage over His first followers.

But to avoid misunderstanding we must make a distinction. For in regard to miracles two questions are involved, one as to whether certain recorded events actually happened, and the second as to what interpretation is to be put on those that are believed to have happened. An event, no matter how rare or wonderful, is not a miracle in any sense that concerns us here, unless it is taken as an overriding of natural order which proves divine activity. The beginning of every personality is a supremely wonderful event, but no one regards it as a miracle in the sense in which the virgin-birth is generally claimed to be so. It is true that believers in the virgin-birth of Jesus have sometimes maintained that it is not an unparalleled occurrence ; but this is really an attempt to prove that it was not a miracle but a monstrosity.

Of course, there is a strong connection between the nature of the interpretation we put on an event of this sort and our willingness to accept its historicity, but it makes for honesty to keep the two aspects as separate as possible. Whether we believe that a recorded fact actually happened must be determined by the evidence, which must be strong in proportion as the fact is unusual. And, of course, it must be remembered that what we deem unusual is so only in relation to what we know, and that further knowledge may show it to be less unusual: in this way the recent recognition of the therapeutic power of suggestion affects greatly the credibility of the works of healing attributed to Jesus.

In the last section we considered the attitude of those who, with the avowed object of making indubitable the validity of Jesus' revelation of God, insist upon miraculous elements as evidence that He was essentially other than we are. We saw that this attitude involved the assumption that apart from Jesus we have assured knowledge of God, by which we must therefore validate His divinity. To anyone who first finds sureness of God through Jesus the whole situation is reversed. All that in Jesus makes us sure of God is bound up with the assumption that He is not essentially or ideally different from us in origin, manhood, or relationship to God. It is His moral splendour as a man that gives our faith its conscious vitality. But human goodness cannot exist without the possibility of sin, and this could not be attributed to one who had pre-existed as God.

It is sometimes said that Jesus was a moral miracle and that such unique goodness proves that He was not merely man. This implies that the goodness of Jesus was essentially impossible to humanity. But a goodness that is essentially impossible to humanity is not humanly good. If I say, " Here is a quality which proves that this animal is not a horse," it shows that I am speaking of a quality that has no place in our conception of a horse and is not part of our ideal of a horse. But it is precisely because Jesus presents us with what is so convincingly the top of all human goodness that He convinces us of the God implied in human goodness. It is only because He is so intensely and completely man that He makes us sure of God.

The attempt to prove that Jesus was other than man obstructs His power to help us. For if He was other than man, then we do not see the truth of our life in Him, and the witness of our conscience to Him is invalidated. If He was other than man, then it is a mistake to see in Him the goal of our direction. It is sometimes suggested that Jesus must be other than man, if He is to reveal God truly and authentically. But if God is the truth of life, then to say that man cannot reveal Him is to say that the truth of life is something foreign to our being, so that when humanity is true to itself it is a stranger to the truth of life. But we can neither think that God desired our distance from the truth, nor that He cannot help it in us, for He did help it in Jesus. On the other hand, if humanity, in proportion as it is true to itself, gets near to the truth of life, then we need only be sure of the utterly true manhood of Jesus and we shall see God in Him.

The availability of Jesus' thought of God for us depends upon its being a man's thought of God. His perfect religious life, i.e. His relationship as man to God, is unintelligible if it was really the relationship of God to God. For what God is to God we can never know. And if it could be shown that Jesus' thought of God was not man's thought of God but God's thought of Himself, then His thought of God could have no meaning for us, and the whole manner and content of Jesus' sayings would be belied, for He always spoke as man of God.

It may perhaps be said that this makes it impossible for God to reveal Himself to man at all. If what God is to God cannot find place in man's mind,

how can God make known His thoughts to man ?
To which the answer must be that God can reveal
Himself to man only by incarnating Himself in man.
For how can man ever know God in any degree truly
and surely otherwise than by virtue of something
divine in man ?

From this point of view we see that the doctrine
of incarnation is necessary to the gospel and is determined by it. If we contend that, by virtue of the
incarnation of God in Jesus, He was essentially other
than man, then He took life on other terms than we
take it, and the moral pull of His life upon ours is
uncoupled. If Jesus remembered being God, then
it was easy for Him to be loyal and courageous. If,
being God, He was not conscious of it, then His consciousness of self was radically inadequate to the
truth, and therefore His conscious acts were not truly
self-expressive.

On the other hand, if God can reveal Himself to
man only by incarnating Himself in man, then He
must ever have sought incarnation in humanity, and
we must regard the incarnation of God in man as
the essential element in human nature. Here we find
the one thing we are sure of in ourselves,—the direction that is truly ours whether we take it or not, the
ideal, unfaithfulness to which makes us untrue to
ourselves. Just so far as men fall short of this
ideal, they are broken, imperfect, hindered, defeated,
perverted incarnations of God. We find the full
and true incarnation of God in Jesus because He
is truer man than any of us, because He is the one
true Man.

This view sees Jesus as the culmination of the
whole evolutionary process, which is thus the travail
of God's incarnation at length achieved in Him.
And this view removes a difficulty, for as long as we

regard the incarnation of God as a solitary act, the rest of human history offers an obstacle to our understanding and reception of it. For though all Christian thought grants that God did in Jesus what He did in no other, the miraculous view of incarnation assumes that God had not been trying to do it in others. This implies that the world, apart from or at least before Jesus, is a world of men and women for whose good God did not do all that He might have done, and so it stands as a contradiction to Jesus' thought of God.

(5)

One of the necessities of modern Christian thought is to relate the doctrine of incarnation to the doctrine of evolution. The doctrine of incarnation by miraculous intervention was, as we have seen, hardly avoidable in pre-evolutionary thinking. If we think of the world and all existing species of life as having been created by a quick succession of divine fiats and then left to continue by themselves without such intensity of divine operation as created them and without possibility of creative change, then we cannot do justice to the creative personality of Jesus without regarding it as the result of a special divine act. In this case the incarnation must stand in sharp discontinuity with the preceding processes of the world.

But if we accept the theory of evolution and think of God's work in the world as continuous, then we must regard His incarnation in Jesus as being related to the preceding evolutionary process as closely as the preceding stages are related to each other. For unless God intended the evolutionary development of life to lead up to the incarnation of Himself in Jesus, He lacks continuity of purpose. But if one divine will and purpose are behind both evolution and incarnation, then the evolutionary process must be regarded as God's means to His incarnation and there will be no break of continuity between them.

We have seen that the idea of Jesus' miraculous origin diminishes the content and validity of His revelation of God. And if such an idea was inevitable to pre-evolutionary thought, it follows that the evolutionary theory enables us for the first time to think of Jesus in a way that does justice to His unique religious significance without diminishing His moral splendour.

But though the doctrine of evolution makes the idea of Jesus' miraculous origin untenable, we find many who attempt to hold to both. Those who do so generally argue that before God could become incarnate in man, man must become a spiritual being, and his moral and spiritual development must reach a certain stage. They explain that God became incarnate in a Jew because the Jews had developed morally and spiritually beyond others. And they look upon Jesus as standing at the culmination of this peculiar racial development.

When we ask, " Why then stipulate for a different origin for Jesus ? " the answer will be, " Because He was sinless and all the rest were sinners." It is not the intellectual powers of Jesus but the sinlessness of His will that is held to demand the theory of special divine origin. That is, it is acknowledged that the evolutionary process produces men who do not differ essentially from the actually incarnate Son of God except in the will. But the will is not a thing that can be made good or bad by any power other than itself. No will, human or divine, can compel another to be good, for goodness must be voluntary if it is to be real. So that the essential difference which is said to exist between the acknowledged products of evolution and the incarnate Son of God is one that the power of God cannot produce.

Hence comes the contention that it was not due to God's power exercised upon a man, but was due to the fact that God Himself was miraculously incarnate in Jesus, i.e. the will of Jesus was sinless because it was a divine and not merely a human will. But here we come upon the very difficult question, " How can the will of Jesus be a human will at all if He was God ? " The Church early and rightly repudiated the idea (which is nevertheless quite common amongst Christians who think themselves orthodox) that Jesus was God in a human body only. And we recognize that the whole content of His revelation of God depends upon His having a human will. But we have seen the last of the psychology in which a man had a will as he had a suit of clothes and might conceivably have two wills, a human and a divine. To us the will is the man willing : the will is the expression of the whole personality. So that to stipulate that a certain being is in origin essentially different from man is to make it inconceivable that he should have a human will. There are at least two insuperable difficulties in the idea of a being who is held to have both an essentially divine will and a truly human will. We have first the difficulty that his human will could not have expressed his whole personality, and therefore could not, properly speaking, be a will at all. Then there is the problem as to how the divine will in him could make the human will good without destroying freedom and so making any sort of real goodness impossible.

There is but one possible conception of unity between the divine will and the human will, i.e. when we think of them as two distinct wills of two distinct personalities willing the same thing. And further

we have to think that the human will is not compelled to will the same as the divine will, otherwise
there would not be two wills but only one, the divine.
If we believe that Jesus pre-existed as God, we cannot
think of Him as having a human will unless we are
prepared to return to a long obsolete psychology.
The will is the characteristic activity of the whole
personality, of the whole man. And an essential
element in man is the part that evolution has played
in producing him. So that the will of a differently
produced being is not human in any way that is
significant for us, and to posit such an origin in order
to account for a sinless man is only to confess that He
could not have been man at all in any real sense.

If we say that Jesus could not have been mere
man because He was sinless, we imply that man cannot
help sinning. But is it sin to do what we cannot
help doing? And if it be replied that it was once
possible for man, but that the fall made it impossible,
then we are supposing that man was once at a higher
stage of moral and spiritual development than at the
time of the incarnation. And this brings the difficulty
of supposing either that a certain degree of depravity
was necessary before Jesus was possible or that God
might have intervened earlier and did not.

These are a few of the difficulties involved in the
attempt to fit the traditional pre-evolutionary Christology into the doctrine of evolution.

On the other hand, if we first get an assured knowledge of God in Jesus, and if God is the underlying
truth of all life, then it follows that to do justice to
Jesus' revelation we must regard Him as essentially
related to the whole process of evolutionary life. He
is its interpreter. The ultimate reality behind all
life explains itself in Him. We thus interpret the
antecedents of Jesus in the light of His own truth.

For God as we know Him in Jesus seeks all men and would enter into all lives to the utmost, so that the history of human development is the history of God's endeavour to incarnate Himself in man. And if He does not enter all lives equally, it is because He cannot : there is a bar on their side. And this bar is twofold : if God was not to all men what He was to Jesus, it was partly because man had not grown to sufficient stature of mind and heart to understand God as Jesus understood Him, and partly because no man was ever before willing to commit himself entirely to what he did know of God. And the unwillingness depended partly on the immaturity, for a partial knowledge of God lacks moral power. And we have also to recognize that the unwillingness of any man to do the right creates an additional difficulty for all with whom he has to do.

Christianity, by the place it accords to Hebrew Scripture, acknowledges that we cannot understand Jesus apart from the history that preceded Him and from the needs and hopes of humanity. But this, for modern ears, is tantamount to saying that we cannot understand Him apart from the evolutionary process of human development. It, without Him, is an unanswered question : He, without it, speaks to our need in an unknown tongue.

It is impossible to attempt an exhaustive exposition of this question. Much work has yet to be done by many minds before we see the full significance of Jesus in the evolution of humanity. All that we can attempt is to give a few suggestions with regard to the final stages of the process that immediately preceded the coming of Jesus.[1]

And here we must notice a common mistake. It

[1] For certain other considerations in this connection see the author's *Essays in Christian Thinking*, chaps. xii, xiii, xiv, and xviii.

is often assumed that by an evolutionary process is meant one that proceeds only in one direction by a gradual accumulation of imperceptible differences. And connected with this is the equally mistaken assumption that when persons are considered in connection with the evolution of humanity, they are thought of as being made what they were by accepting the common thoughts of their day. Of course, no person who was in any sense unique could be part of such a process, nor has it room for genius of any sort. We have to remember that it is now generally acknowledged that evolution, even on the lower levels of life, is not always by imperceptible differences, and that such a conception of it is grotesquely inadequate to the historically observable process of development in the moral and religious life of humanity at its higher stages.

The most significant of the later steps in the religious development of humanity is the appearance of universal religions as distinct from national religions. In national religions each cult is proper to some particular nation or race and to it only. The god or set of gods is regarded as the god or gods of that one nation only, which is their particular realm and care : the land is often regarded as their property and they are to be worshipped most acceptably at certain sacred places in it. The religion at this stage is an indigenous product of racial life. Its incidence is national rather than individual. It is the centre and symbol of national life. Of this type are the religions of most of the great nations of antiquity : it persists in India and China. We are most familiar with it in the earlier stages of Hebrew religion. But out of these national religions there arose in several places religions which claimed man as man without distinction of race. Of such are Zoroastrianism,

Buddhism, Christianity, Islam. In contrast with the national religions these have all been founded by great personalities. Their appeal is both universal and personal. They are free from rigid attachment to holy places, though on this point Islam's Mecca must be excepted. It is unquestionable that this development to the universal in religion marks an advance, and that nothing but a universal religion can now satisfy the religious needs of humanity.

A second element upon which the more highly developed religious need of mankind insists is that religion must be ethical. A religion that is not vitally related to conduct cannot command the allegiance of adult humanity. And ultimately the only acceptable ethics is that of loving our neighbour as ourselves. National religion could, and did in the case of Judaism, climb as high as this, so long as "neighbour" was interpreted as fellow-countryman. But obviously a universal religion needed the wider interpretation that Jesus gave the word in the parable of the good Samaritan and in the command to love our enemies. In all thoughtful ethics, and therefore in a truly universal religion, the "neighbour" whom we must love as ourselves has to include all personalities. We have here the culminating step in the development of ethics analogous to the advance from the national to the universal religion. And it is significant that in the religion of Jesus, and apparently in that only, these two advances are made simultaneously and are recognized as vital to each other. He taught the Jews that the way to be children of their heavenly Father was to love their enemies (Matt. v. 43–48).

History shows that the advance from the national to the universal is the normal line of development along which religion, when it reaches a certain point, must move, if its vigour is to be retained. History also shows that this transition does not occur by imperceptible degrees but generally by means of sharpest conflict. The old does not usually pass smoothly into the new, but repudiates and persecutes it. This accounts for the fact that at this stage the forward movement depends on the initiative and valour of great personalities. Yet these forceful men, who break with the past and initiate the new, are in certain important respects the product of the past. These considerations apply also to advances in the higher levels of ethical development. Here, too, advance is generally made good only by struggle between the old and the new, a struggle in which the sincerest upholders of the old good are often the most determined enemies of the new. Here, too, the new is often initiated by the insight of outstanding characters and is made good only by their endurance.

Amongst the founders of the universal religions Jesus stands alone. Of Zoroaster we know little, and his religion seems moribund. Mohammed is in point of character not comparable with Jesus : his sex relationships and his conduct towards his enemies are not of the highest. It is, of course, unfair to judge him as a man without making allowance for his time and place, but, in considering him as the founder of a religion, this only reminds us that the significance of a religious genius is bound up with the moral and religious significance of his race.

Gautama in character and in intellect stands above Mohammed. Yet his abandonment of his wife was a breach of contract that is not easy to justify. And when we compare him with Jesus, we cannot but mark that the story of his struggle shows him concerned for his own peace of mind and his own escape from suffering in a way of which we find no trace in

Jesus. We must not shut our eyes to the fact that, despite certain resemblances, Gautama and Jesus stand in sharp contrast with each other. We may compare their attitude towards disease. We see, too, that had the Buddha found Jesus weeping over Jerusalem, he would have bade Him be rid of this sorrow by uprooting the desire from which it grew. Jesus would thus have found in Buddha's doctrine a subtler repetition of that which evoked His rebuke to Peter, " Get thee behind me Satan, for thou mindest not the things of God, but the things of men." And we are reminded that to Buddha the gods were of no importance. The comparison, however, will be more illuminating if seen in broader setting.

A normal stage in the development of religions is one in which the deity is regarded as the punisher of iniquity and the rewarder of righteousness. This faith is characteristic of the national stage of religion. God is thought of as lawgiver and judge and vindicator of the commonweal.

When once this stage is reached, the factors involved indicate that further development can be expected only along two lines, the pursuit of which was carried with thoroughness to their respective issues by Gautama and Jesus.[1] These two lines of development diverge at the question as to whether punishment and reward are God's fundamental reaction towards man or not. The belief that they are finds

[1] Islam is in this respect anomalous. By means of material indirectly absorbed in an impure form from Judaism and Christianity, Mohammed passed straight from a tribal to a universal religion, omitting the normally intermediate national stage. The result is that Islam, though universal in form, has the characteristic contents of national religion,—God is supremely lawgiver and judge. In Islam also Church and State are one, Mohammed's ideal not being that of a religion that should be indifferent to political distinctions, but that of a religious society that should absorb all states. Lastly, it has the surest mark of the national level in religious thought, a supremely holy place, Mecca.

its logical issue in the teaching of Buddha. Israel had tendencies in this direction, as is witnessed by the importance of the covenant in the later development of their religion. But this development was hindered by the Hebrew sense of fact, which brought them (in " Job " and elsewhere) to question the universal equivalence of suffering and sin. It was also opposed by the intensity of their devotion, which could not be satisfied with a divine paymaster. The dominating idea of a divine lawgiver and judge, however, persisted and showed its normal concomitant in the intense nationalism of the Pharisaic stage.

In the Buddha we find the idea of God as supremely Rewarder and Punisher carried to its logical conclusion. The Indian religion into which Gautama was born tended towards pantheism and lacked the intensely ethical and personal deity of Israel. The belief in the transmigration of souls attributed discrepancies of fortune to the supposed merits or demerits of a former life and thus masked the contradictions with which the facts of life oppose belief in a divinely ordained and perfect system of punishment and reward. This doctrine of Karma was the only religious belief of his day that Gautama made an effective part of his system, of which it was the fundamental axiom. It gives an inexorable and impersonal form to the belief that the dominant reaction of God to human action is in reward and punishment. It makes the supreme element of man's contact with reality to be its power of causing him pain. It makes his one concern to escape pain. But this implies that there is a fundamental diversity between man's good and any divine purpose that may be attributed to the universe,—Gautama apparently recognized none. Prayer can do nothing for man : there is no fellowship possible between him and God, not even so much as to make sin possible. For though Gautama speaks of right and wrong, the fundamental difference between them, so far as he is concerned, is that wrong brings pain to the doer and right does not. And since all pain is occasioned by desire, man's salvation lies in the extinction of all desire, so that he must withdraw himself from all natural bonds and activities into ascetic celibacy.

Such an outcome indicates an initial mistake, and the point at which the wrong step was made has already been indicated. The doctrine of transmigration of souls made rigid and universal the morally and religiously immature idea that the supreme concern of God with man was to punish sin with pain and to reward righteousness with pleasure. This idea implies that, from the divine side of things, human morality is seen to be nothing but fear of pain and love of pleasure, i.e. not to be truly moral at all. In telling us that God must bribe or threaten man into the doing of the divine will it implies that God's concern and man's are not the same. This implied antagonism between the human and the divine involves also an antagonism between the universe and man, between life and self-consciousness, and these antagonisms, obscured at first, became clear to the strong intelligence of Gautama.

This wrong step was taken in India because it followed logically upon the idea of God as judge and lawgiver, which is normal at a certain stage in religious development, and because India was logical rather than moral. For India, as we have seen, lacked that intensity of ethical spirit which drove the higher minds of Israel beyond the ideas of the covenant with its stipulation of conditional rewards and punishments.

One of the most notable things in the later development of Hebrew religion was Jeremiah's recognition of the failure and insufficiency of the covenant. And the connection of suffering with sin which was the very base of the covenant is questioned and denied from different points of view in Job and Isa. liii. And from what has just been considered, it is clear that the command (which Jesus saw to be greatest of all), the command to love God whole-heartedly, is incompatible with the idea that God's fundamental relation to man is that of punisher and rewarder. We have thus in Israel's religious development a trend of thought and experience which, starting from the idea of God as lawgiver and judge, came to feel that this idea was radically inadequate.

But to deny that punishment and reward are the fundamental and dominant reaction of God to human act is to make the tremendous assumption that the desires of God and man may be, and ought to be, essentially at one with each other. It assumes that God's ends and man's highest good are one, and that man can see them to be one, and therefore that when man knows himself he sees righteousness to be his proper good apart from all punishment or reward. And such an idea of fellowship and loyalty and voluntary co-operation between God and man carries with it the need of thinking of God as possessing personality. For there can be true unity of desire between God and man only if God is thought of as loving man supremely and being Himself supremely lovable Man is reconciled to life, self-consciousness is reconciled with reality, only when the fundamental reality is conceived of as a God whom man can love " with all his heart and mind and soul and strength." And we have seen that Jesus was the first to give man a thought of a God that man could so love. Jesus stands at the culmination of that trend of the development of Hebrew religion which avoided the false step that India took. He is thus seen to stand at the head of the whole process of the world's religious development.

In Him we have the affirmation of the fundamental kinship of self-consciousness and reality, of man and God. His discipline is not that desire should be suppressed but that it should be purified from self-bias (as in the Golden Rule) and intensified into a divinely magnanimous love. Jesus' thought of God gives to man an idea of the fundamental reality that for the first time in history makes the universe his home. Otherwise man, nature's greatest and most elaborated product, is an orphan, a misfit, an anomaly, an absurdity in the universe that produced him.

We see thus that the work of Jesus appears in the closest and most essential connection with the whole process of human evolution. To consider Him as an extraneous insertion into human history is wantonly to diminish and obscure His significance. It would seem rather that in Him, at length, life came to full consciousness of itself and full awareness of its divine secret. " In Him was life ; and the life was the light of men."

But it may be asked, " On such a view how do you account for the fact that life paused here and produced no more such men as Jesus ? " In other words, how, from the evolutionary point of view, can we account for the uniqueness of Jesus ? It is, of course, impossible to explain any human being, but it is possible to indicate conditions that show Jesus to be essentially related to the past and future evolution of the race in a way that does make Him unique. It is not difficult to see what is needed to fulfil this requirement. We need to find conditions of life that produce a continually higher and higher type of man until the highest possible point is reached ; we need also to find that when that point is reached, and by the reaching of it, the conditions that led up to it cease to be active, and further these conditions must be of the sort that cannot recur. If the historic conditions under which Jesus appeared can be shown to be of this kind, then His very place in the development of humanity will secure His uniqueness.

In order to produce a morally and religiously ascending series of men, there must be a long continuity of social life moved by a persistent and intense moral and religious ideal, and there must be freedom from the corrupting influence of lower types of social life. This we have in Israel.[1] Never has any race been so long and so intensely moved by moral and religious ideals as Israel in the centuries before Jesus. And the Hebrews, conscious that their religion and morality were the purest and highest in the world, guarded them by avoiding all mixture with other nations and by repudiating all alien morals and religion. And this history did produce an ascending series of men,—Amos, Hosea, Jeremiah, the author of the latter part of Isaiah, the authors of the later Psalms, and he of whom Jesus said that none greater had been born of woman. And we have here conditions that can hardly occur again. For unless their religion had really been the highest in the world, their belief that it was so and their segregation could not have had the result that it did have in morals and religion. And such social segregation and intensive social culture of religion can take place only when religion is at what is recognized as the " national " stage. It is obviously impossible with a universal or missionary religion. But it is also clear that the

[1] For other suggestions as to the working of this process see the author's *Essays in Christian Thinking*, pp. 180 ff.

highest type of religion and ethics is universal, and that such must be the ethics and religion of the highest type of man. It would seem, therefore, that the highest Man can appear only under certain conditions, i.e. at the culmination of the highest national religion, and that when He appears He will, if His faithfulness matches His opportunity, lift the national religion into a universal one and will thus inaugurate an era in which the intensive process at the culmination of which He stands will pass into an expansive and invasive movement. He will destroy the national segregation that made Him possible and will prevent its recurrence. So that the conditions under which such a man appears can occur but once.

These considerations have another aspect. In tracing moral advance in the race, probably the most important element is the growth of the altruistic side of human nature. Love is the fulfilling of the law. And at a certain well-marked stage of human history the altruistic side of human nature has its highest feature in patriotism. In scope patriotism is short only of love of humanity, which it commonly exceeds in intensity. Now at the typically national stage of religion patriotism and religion are one, and there is, within these limits, an almost perfect fusion of religion and ethics. But it is clear that if the next step,—from the national to the universal,—is to be taken without loss, the fire of patriotism must be carried into the service of humanity. This means that the national ideal must find its fulfilment in the service of the world, which can take place with fullest religious significance only where a nation finds it has a religion that can serve the world's need. It would seem then from this point of view also that such a one as Jesus could find the conditions of His being only where the highest of national religions passes into the highest universal religion. It is also obvious that the Man who mediates this transition will be of unique significance in religion, and, further, that such an occasion can happen but once in the history of the world.

(6)

But we have yet to consider a very special factor in the uniqueness of Jesus. The process of growth by which humanity rose to the moral and intellectual level that made Him possible was complicated and strained by man's unwillingness to act by the light he had. And the unwillingness of others makes it much harder for anyone to do so, and so makes more stringent and exacting the conditions for a true incarnation of God. Here we pass from what is usually included under the theology of the person of Jesus to that of His work.

When we remember that it was both human immaturity and human unwillingness that denied God a true and full incarnation until He found it in Jesus, we have a further answer to those who tell us that, if we see Jesus as the consummation of the evolutionary process, then the process has retrograded since His day. For if the incarnation of God does not depend only upon maturity of human development, but has to contend with the unwillingness of men, then His full incarnation in the highest Man will have to be intense and active and powerful in proportion to the world's degree of unwillingness. And since the unwillingness of men is partly conditioned by the inadequacy of their knowledge of God, it follows that when once, in spite of human opposition, God is truly made known, the unwillingness can never again be so universal or intense. Therefore there can never again be conditions for so heroic an advocacy of God.

It is in the sheer heroism rather than in the mere sinlessness of Jesus that we find the uniqueness of God's incarnation in Him. After Jesus, in the fight of right with wrong, His followers have never to face the odds He found. His faithfulness and His victory give them an advantage that He lacked.

This consideration shows the connection between Jesus' uniqueness and His work. If we regarded only His place at a great historic crisis, where national development of an unparalleled sort culminated in making possible a man of unique moral and religious genius, we might regard Him as a specially favoured individual, so happily constituted by heredity and environment as to find it easier than others to be good. But when we see the task to which He was set by virtue of what He was, we see that the very greatness of His heritage and the very loftiness of His soul brought Him to problems and struggles and temptations harder and fiercer than those of which smaller men are capable. We see that, whatever was His by heredity, all would have been lost without the will to do and to suffer to the uttermost. The unique greatness of His soul was matched by the unique hardness of His task.

It is not necessary here to repeat how the Jewish opposition to Jesus' endeavour for the kingdom of God accentuated His consciousness of being solitary in His knowledge of God (Matt. xi. 20–27, Luke x. 13–22) and compelled Him to direct His followers' thoughts to Himself (Mark viii. 27 ff). We need only review in a little more detail the relationship of His death to His life's work.

The coming of the kingship of God which Jesus preached must ultimately depend upon the power of God's goodness to overcome the evil of man's heart and evoke his willing loyalty. The characteristic of

Jesus' teaching was that God was not merely good but that His goodness was of the intense, initiative, invasive kind that sought the wanderer and loved the ungrateful and evil. It is precisely here that His thought of God was new to the world, and here, as we have seen, it has just that redemptive quality for lack of which lesser thoughts of God lack power and credibility. It was in the service of the gospel of this goodness in God that Jesus went to death. This becomes clearer the more we consider His death in its historic circumstances. And the more we see the inevitableness of this connection, the surer we shall be of the futility of any explanation of Jesus' death that ignores it.

The story makes it clear that there are two distinguishable aspects of Jesus' sufferings. On the one hand, we see that He encountered death as a means to the purpose for which He lived. On the other hand, it is clear that in His final suffering there was something from which He shrank, something that implies a sense of failure more bitter than death. We have it in the agony of Gethsemane and in the cry, " Why hast Thou forsaken Me ? " Here is something in His death that cannot be explained as a means to the end for which He lived. For it is impossible that one who expected by His death to gain what was dearer to Him than life should be overwhelmed by agony of spirit.

With regard to the first aspect, we see that Jesus met His death in His appointed and accepted task of making God king of the hearts of men. And He Himself chose deliberately the issue on which He should die. No interpretation of His death is legitimate that does not give just place to the fact that it resulted directly from the challenge which He gave to the religious authorities of Jerusalem by the

cleansing of the Temple. It was this that moved the
chief priests to compass His death. In the influence
of the religious authorities He found the greatest
obstacle to Israel's acceptance of His truth, and here
He came to issue with this obstacle. He would free
His people from it, would " give His life a ransom
for many." And this was the actual result of His
death. His followers were freed from the influence
and prestige of priest and scribe who had killed Him,
as is abundantly evident in the early chapters of
Acts. The regular use of Jesus' death in the earliest
recorded preaching was to discredit the greatest
opposing force with which the followers of Jesus had
to contend (see pp. 39 and 86).

But there was more in the incident than this.
Jesus not only drove the sellers from the Temple, but
assumed control of it for a time and taught that it
was intended by God to be a house of prayer for all
nations (Mark xi. 16, 17). The significance of this is
that the Temple was the centre and symbol of all
that was most intensely national in Hebrew religion.
It was the sanctuary of their patriotism.

Many things show that the result of Jesus' preaching
to His people had not been what He hoped for and
expected. His upbraiding of unrepentant Galilee
(Matt. xi. 20–24, Luke x. 13–15) and His tears over
Jerusalem (Luke xix. 41) are evidence of hope unfulfilled. The greatness of His expectation is seen in
" The harvest is plenteous " (Matt. ix. 37, Luke x. 2)
and in the parable of the sower, where the unfruitful
seed is a negligible quantity beside the abundance of
return. His message, " Repent ye," was to the nation,
and we must suppose that He saw the possibility of
that for which He called. The number of the Twelve
is the number of Israel's tribes, and He promised that
they should sit on thrones judging the twelve tribes

of Israel (Luke xxii. 30). The Israelites are to Him
" the sons of the kingdom " (Matt. viii. 12) : Jeru-
salem is " the city of the Great King " (Matt. v. 35).
And when we take into consideration the largeness of
His view, perhaps the most significant evidence that
His call to repentance was national is found in His
confining His own work and the immediate work of
His followers to Israel (Matt. x. 5, 6 ; xv. 24).

For it is certain that, if Jesus' preaching was
limited to Israel, His purview was not. In Luke's
first account of His teaching Jesus angers the Naza-
renes by reminding them of God's care for the Gentiles
(Luke iv. 25–29), He compares Galilee unfavourably
with Tyre and Sidon (Matt. xi. 21, Luke x. 13), and
the Jews with the Ninevites and the Queen of the
South (Matt. xii. 41, 42 ; Luke xi. 31, 32). He found
greater faith in the Gentile centurion than in any
Jew (Matt. viii. 10, Luke vii. 9). He foresaw the
Gentiles assembling in the kingdom of God (Matt. viii.
11, Luke xiii. 28). The term most frequently on His
lips, " the kingdom of God," took the world into its
embrace, and the term which He so often applied to
Himself, " the Son of man," had the same super-
national scope (cf. Dan. vii. 13, 14, 18, 27). Bearing
these things in mind, we are led to conclude that the
outstanding thing in the repentance or " change of
mind " to which He would bring Israel as a nation
was a change from despising and hating the Gentiles
to serving them by giving them the truth of God.
The only sign He would promise to Israel was that of
Jonah to the Ninevites, the sign of a Jew preaching
to Gentiles (Matt. xii. 39, xvi. 4 ; Luke xi. 29). To
the Syrophœnician woman He said, " Let the children
first be filled." His criticism of the ethics of His
people in comparison with the demands of the kingdom
of God culminates in the command to love their

enemies (Matt. v. 43 ff.). And it is fairly clear from the passage which He cites (Lev. xix. 18, where " neighbour " is fellow Israelite) that " enemy " here means especially " Gentile " (cf. Deut. xxiii. 3–6). And His all-inclusive interpretation of " neighbour " is given in the parable of the good Samaritan.

The recognition of this significant element of His appeal throws light on many passages of His life and teaching. His controversy with the Jews as to the law generally concerned those things, such as Sabbath observance, ceremonial washings, clean and unclean foods, which made for exclusiveness and prevented the Jew from mixing with the Gentile. His relation to the publicans, who served Rome and were therefore repudiated by their fellow Jews, was another matter of contention. The parable of the vineyard labourers (Matt. xx. 1 ff.) meets those who boasted of a covenant with God, which the Gentiles lacked, and who asked if it was fair that the Gentiles, who had not borne the burden and heat of the day, should now share with the Jew the blessings of the kingdom of God. The servant who defended his profitless seclusion of the entrusted talent on the plea of his lord's strictness would describe aptly the attitude of the exclusive Jew towards his entrusted truth and the world's need (Matt. xxv. 24, 25 ; Luke xix. 20, 21). It seems likely that Matt. v. 13, 14, " Ye are the salt of the earth . . . Ye are the light of the world," was addressed to Jews as such, and was a call to them to fulfil their prophetic destiny (Isa. xl. 6, xlix. 6, lx. 3), for the words " . . . if the salt have lost its savour . . ." are much more applicable to Jews as such than to the followers of Jesus. And to the Jew the " city set on a hill " could not but suggest Jerusalem.

Jesus could not have inherited the highest moral

qualities of His race without sharing their consuming
patriotism. But He certainly did not share the
patriotism that dreamt of a world-dominance for
Israel by force of arms divine or human. His ideal
of dominance was service. And it can hardly be
doubted that He longed with all His heart to see His
people fulfil their foretold destiny of being a light to
the Gentiles. It is, in this connection, of the highest
significance that the voice that came to Him at
baptism, " Thou art My beloved Son, in Thee I am
well pleased," is directly reminiscent of a scripture
(Isa. xlii.1–9 ; cf. vs. 1 and 6) that speaks of the servant
of God, " My chosen, in whom My soul delighteth "
as " a light of the Gentiles." This evinces Jesus'
dominant thought at the moment of consecration to
His divine mission. And in the stir of thought that
follows, He is thinking of " all the kingdoms of the
world " (Matt. iv. 8, Luke iv. 5). The action, too,
which, in the parable of the vineyard, He describes
as God's final demand from Israel for the fruit of their
trust (Mark xii. 1–9) was the cleansing of the court of
the Gentiles and the occupancy of the Temple by
One who called Himself " the Son of man " and who
demanded that it should be " a house of prayer for
all the Gentiles " (Mark xi. 16, 17).

And Jesus saw that here, as so often elsewhere in
history, great possibility of good was bound up with
great possibility of evil. His people's great opportunity was their judgment day : to refuse His call
was to seal their own doom. Hence the urgency of
His message. " Agree with thine adversary quickly,
whiles thou art with him in the way . . ." (Matt. v.
25, 26 ; Luke xii. 58, 59). " Except ye repent, ye shall
all likewise perish " (Luke xiii. 1–5). " Let it alone
this year also . . . and if it bear fruit, well ; but if
not thou shalt cut it down " (Luke xiii. 6–9). And

when their rejection of Him became more patent, His forecast of doom became more definite,—" It shall be required of this generation " (Matt. xxiii. 36, Luke xi. 51) : " Weep not for Me, but weep for yourselves " (Luke xxiii. 27 ff.).

Passages like those just cited (together with others like Mark xiii. 2, 14 ff. ; Luke xiii. 1–5, xx. 41–44) make it highly probable that Jesus foresaw the war between Israel and Rome. Indeed, it is difficult to see how any intelligent Jew could have been blind to the imminent possibility. Jesus urged the intense patriotism of Israel to find its destiny in giving light to the world, but Israel chose what appears to have been the only alternative to its pent forces,—rebellion against Rome. Jesus' final appeal was refused, and as He left the Temple to be reoccupied by its customary guardians, He foretold its complete destruction (Mark xiii. 1, 2) and addressed Himself to the death which was now the only alternative to unfaithfulness and the only hope of breaking the religious influence of His adversaries.

The chief circumstance that led to the death of Jesus thus appears to have been His attempt to lead the religion and ethics of His people from the national stage of development, at the culmination of which they stood, to the universal, at which they might have been " a light to the Gentiles " and so might not only have saved themselves from hopeless struggle with Rome but have flung the enormous impact of their patriotism into the task of establishing God's kingship in the world by making known their truth of God.

And it is clear that this attempt is the direct outcome of what is most characteristic in Jesus' teaching of God. Had the Jews in any positive way attempted to make the Temple " a house of prayer for all the nations," it would have meant that they, like God, must seek the lost and love their enemies. This thought of God was one with the utterness of Jesus' own love for man. He was moved by it to impart it, with all its call and promise, first to His people and through them to the world, and He followed its leading unfalteringly to the death. He was conscious too that He was therein acting for and with God. To Peter's repudiation of His Master's prediction of suffering, Jesus answers, " Thou mindest not the things of God, but the things of men " (Mark viii. 33).

His truth's essential and victorious freedom from all inhuman limits, and the world-wide intent that brought Him to death, make it no more than simply true for us to say, " He died for me." And so upon us comes the impact of the love that accepted and endured the cross and discovered to us its own secret and source in the love of God.

(7)

We have now the second aspect of Jesus' death to consider. We have just seen that He died in contest with priest and scribe and Pharisee in order to free His people from the influence that kept them from accepting His truth. But that intent failed so far as the vast majority of the nation was concerned, and He knew before He died that it had failed. Had He been sure of winning by His death that for which He died, He would have died joyful in spirit as many martyrs have died.

When all had been done that could be done for His followers and He turned in Gethsemane to face at close quarters all that was involved in His death, He was overcome with sorrow. The cry, " My God,

My God, why hast Thou forsaken Me ? " tells us that this mortal sorrow mounted the cross with Him. And since He died long before crucifixion could be expected to end life (Mark xv. 44), we are left to conclude that He spoke exactly when He called it " sorrow unto death," and that it was sorrow that killed Him. Nor need we doubt the cause. He had endeavoured to make God, the God He knew, king of the hearts of men. His nation had rejected His truth and chosen the road that must lead to ruin at the hands of Rome. He was forsaken, denied, betrayed by His nearest followers. He had failed in that for which He had lived. His disciples might repent their desertion : He believed they would ; but for the vast majority of His people He knew that their rejection of Him, His truth, His God, was final. Men had denied Him the thing dearer to Him than life, and dearer to Him than life because He knew it to be dearer than life to God. The sorrow that killed Him was the sorrow He shared with God ; it was the cup His Father gave Him to drink. And therefore in this sorrow there was no help for Him in God, a conclusion which gives us the only tolerable explanation of the cry, " Why hast Thou forsaken me ? " (see pp. 45 ff.).

It is here that we get the surest insight into the utterness of Jesus' love, and here, therefore, that His thought of God puts on the height of its power. If, when a man fails in some pursuit, he is consolable, then it was not the dearest thing in the world to him ; for all we know, there may be some reserve of self-love. But when failure kills with sorrow, then we know surely that the man was all love for the thing he sought. And when in such sorrow the man finds no consolation in God, it must be because he knows that God seeks the same thing with the same intensity and self-abandonment of love. Jesus died because human life could not support fellowship with God's sorrow at the world's rejection of the divine love and thwarting of the divine good will.

And so in the death of Jesus God's love found an expression and instrument, which, when men awoke to its significance and felt the spell of its power, enthroned Him in their hearts. It assured them of God's complete unselfishness and so overcame the self-love that withheld them from whole-hearted loyalty to the right. It fired them with a devotion that counted no cost.

It may be objected that this view supposes that it is God's pain at failure that wins Him triumph, i.e. that God triumphs because He could not foresee His triumph. To this it must be answered in the first place that the ultimate triumph was a limited one. Jesus' work and death is unintelligible unless we suppose Him to have believed that a larger response to His call was possible than was actually made. In the Christian Church there were from the first but few and ultimately none of His own people. And He had attempted to win His people as a whole and through them to win the whole world. Even through the rosiest glasses the last nineteen centuries can hardly be looked on as the realization of the possibilities which Jesus acclaimed when He preached that the kingdom of God was at hand. And if Jesus was truly representative of God and was God's utmost appeal, His failure was God's failure too.

But if Jesus was truly representative of God and was justified in expecting and hoping for what did not happen, then God expected and hoped for it too. So at least Jesus thought. He pictures God saying of Him, " They will reverence My Son " (Mark xii. 6), which implies that God did not foresee the rejection of Jesus as something that must necessarily happen. He says, " There shall be joy in heaven over one sinner that repenteth " (Luke xv. 7, 10), and one does not rejoice over a foregone conclusion.

It will be seen here that just as a real moral freedom implies a limitation of divine predestination, it involves also a limitation of divine prescience. For if God from the beginning foresees the end in all its detail with absolute sureness, then nothing in the world can be other than it is, and not only is our moral freedom and moral responsibility a delusion, but the whole time-process of the universe seems a superfluity. The answer may be made that with God there is no past or present, but an eternal now. But if this is so, then, since God is the ultimate reality, we come to the same conclusion,—the time-process with its past and future is unreal. In this case it is difficult to see how Jesus, a man with past and future, living in the time-process, can truly reveal God. If, on the other hand, we take our moral freedom as no delusion, God must be thought of as not having foreclosed all life's possibilities and therefore as capable of disappointment and sorrow. In this case we must think of God as undergoing in Jesus' failure a unique experience of sorrow, for He had found in the life and attempt of Jesus the uniquely adequate revelation of His will and His utmost bid for human loyalty (Mark xii. 6). So that Jesus' " sorrow unto death " once for all reveals the love that is in the heart of God.

These considerations will also help us to meet another objection, for apart from them it might be suggested that the view of Jesus' death set forth here regards it only as a revelation of God and not as an event in which God Himself participated. We see that in the death of Jesus there was a more deeply personal participation of God than even action can afford. God suffered in the suffering of Jesus, or rather it would be more accurate to say that the deepest of Jesus' suffering was His participation of the sorrow of God.

We see thus that, in His death as in His life, Jesus helps and saves us by the thought of God which He gives us. Whatever God did in Jesus, it is through what we think of it that His deed affects us, at least so far as it is of any use to think or speak about it. We can think intelligibly only about the help that God gives to our consciousness, of which by far the most important element must be a true and adequate thought of God. It may perhaps seem as though this implies that God *does* nothing in our salvation. But it is rather that our salvation comes when we recognize the truth of what God is ever doing. God can work in us truly and fully only as we know Him truly. In so far as we are self-conscious beings, it is in our thought of God, and in the activities to which it prompts us, that God's presence in us is most intimate and creative.

The relation of the death of Jesus to the forgiveness of sins has already been discussed (pp. 131 ff.). In the suffering of Jesus we know that God loves us despite our sin and despite the pain with which our sin afflicts His love. We know that our sin does not cancel God's love, and we find that such love makes us hate sin and draws us ever more and more to itself.

We see here a connection between pain borne and sin forgiven. If our sin had caused no pain to God, it would have shown that His love was not great enough to overcome our self-love. For the love that is not pained when it finds selfishness and hate is a poor love. And God's supreme experience of that redemptive pain was in the death of Jesus, the contemplation of which, therefore, more than all else gives us assurance of a love that forgives and restores. But this has no connection whatever with substitutionary or propitiatory sacrifice, and it only obscures thought to pretend that it has.

Such a view of the relation of the death of Jesus to forgiveness has the advantage of being in harmony with His own teaching. This is a condition which should surely be fulfilled by any Christian doctrine, but which is certainly not fulfilled by the idea of forgiveness embodied in the traditional gospel. The significance of the death of Jesus, as we have here viewed it, is simply that in it God's love for sinning man, which was already the master passion of Jesus' life and teaching, had its final and supreme experience and expression.

It may perhaps be said that this view sees only sorrow in God's relationship to sin and leaves no room for the wrath of God even as moral condemnation. But the pain that sin causes to love always contains an element of indignation. Consider the difference between the sorrow of a father whose child suffers and the sorrow of a father whose child has done a shameful or cruel or treacherous thing to his brother or sister. The latter is by far the sharper and deeper sorrow because of an element of moral indignation. If we think of God as concerned only with the suffering caused by sin to the sinner and his fellows, then God's pain at man's wrong-doing is only pity. But if it is sin itself that causes Him pain, then, in that pain, indignation is the most bitter ingredient. And from this it follows that the change from estrangement to forgiveness is not merely a change in the sinner's understanding of God's love. When a man truly repents, God's attitude towards him changes. That is the distinct teaching of Jesus:

" If ye forgive not men their trespasses, neither will your Father forgive your trespasses " (Matt. vi. 15). The difference is not that God's love increases, but that it loses the bitterness of indignation. His fellowship with the man who repents ceases to be a pain : " There is joy in heaven " over the sinner that repents.

(8)

It may perhaps be said that though we have accounted for the uniqueness of Jesus and justified His revelation of God, we have not defined His divinity. Can we speak of Jesus as God ? In considering this question we must remember in the first place that it is absurd to propose it as a test for right thinking about Jesus, since any pantheist might say that Jesus was God.

From all that has been considered here it will appear that the question of Jesus' divinity must be approached along one of two lines :—

(a) If it is in Jesus that we first find an assured knowledge of God, then it is true to say that Jesus is God in the sense that in Him, and in Him only, we see the truth of God. This is, of course, not using language in its strictest sense, although, so used, the words mean more than when we say, " This picture is So-and-so." Indeed, it is in this sense that they have most meaning for our faith.

But it is true also in a more absolute sense. If, in the creation of self-determining men, God limited Himself that He might, in free human fellowship, fulfil Himself, two things follow : (1) Man is divine in essence, for he has his being in the self-limitation of God ; and (2) God, being thus self-limited, is not wholly Himself until His self-limitation achieves its goal. And it achieves its goal only in Jesus. Only in Jesus is God wholly Himself. Only in Jesus does that of God which was imparted to man give itself willingly to God again. So that we may in this sense say absolutely—what we can say of no other man—that Jesus is God. But then, of course, we should be using the word " God " in a different sense from that in which we use it for the heavenly Father to whom Jesus prayed and we should be using it in a sense which is rather dangerous than helpful to religion. For that which makes Jesus unique in this respect is His loyalty to God, and in seeking to do justice to the immense religious importance of that complete loyalty, we must be careful not to obliterate the distinction of personalities on which it depends. For it is the loyalty of One Person to Another, of a Man to God. It is not the loyalty of a self to itself. Jesus was loyal to Himself, but only because He was loyal to One whom He distinguished from Himself. And the moral and religious worth of His oneness with God depends upon the maintenance of this distinctness.

(b) If we take the so-called orthodox position and think that, apart from Jesus, we have an assured knowledge of God, then in saying, " Jesus is God," we think of ourselves as adding to the content of His name. This, of course, means that we are bringing profane fire into the sanctuary and are diluting and qualifying Jesus' interpretation of God by ideas that are not His. Thinking to do honour to Him, we are debasing the coinage of His truth. The usual consequence is that the term so used suggests and implies that Jesus was not truly and simply man, and so obscures the gist and weakens the sureness of His truth.

From the point of view taken here Jesus becomes the central object of our worship and adoration. And it is interesting to see how this reacts on our

PRINTED BY UNWIN BROTHERS, LIMITED, LONDON AND WOKING, GREAT BRITAIN